Best Garden Plants for California

Jennifer Beaver • Don Williamson

LONE PINE

Lone Pine Publishing International

First printed in 2016 10 9 8 7 6 5 4 3 2 1
Printed in China

The Publisher: Lone Pine Publishing
1808 B Street NW, Suite 140
Auburn, WA, USA 98001
Website: www.lonepinepublishing.com

Library and Archives Canada Cataloguing in Publication

Beaver, Jennifer.
Best garden plants for California / Jennifer Beaver, Don Williamson.
pages : color illustrations ; cm

Includes index.
ISBN: 978-976-650-059-7

1. Plants, Ornamental—California. 2. Gardening—California. I. Williamson, Don, 1962– II. Title.

SB453.2.C2 B43 2016 635.9/09794

Photography: All photos by Tamara Eder and Tim Matheson except AARS-2003 118b; AASelection 34a; Allison Penko 10, 53a, 94b, 100b, 105a&b, 132b, 142b, 163a&b, 164a 165b, 166b, 169a&b, 172b; Anne Gordon 138a; Conard-Pyle Roses 113a, 114a; Dawn Loewen 84a; Debra Knapke 138b; Derek Fell, 11a, 80b, 101a&b, 149a, 161a&b; Don Doucette 106b, 134b; Don Williamson 146a&b; Duncan Kelbaugh 145a; Erika Flatt 9c, 74b, 145b, 175b, 171a&b; Gene Sasse-Weeks 113b; Horticolor (G4500059) 133b; Jackson & Perkins 118a; Janet Loughrey 44a; Joy Spurr 129a, 133a; Karen Carriere 51a, 70a; Kim O'Leary 44b, 61b, 75a, 81a, 96a, 99a&b, 147a, 155b; Laura Peters 61a, 73b, 74a, 79b, 81b, 143b, 151a&b, 155a, 156a&b, 157a&b, 158b, 160a, 162b, 164b, 165a, 167a, 170a&b; Leila Sidi 150b; Liz Klose 152a, 153a&b, 158a, 162a, 168a&b, 172a; Marilynn McAra 148a; Mark Turner 79a; Peter Thompstone 22a, 25a, 26a, 31a, 54a, 59a, 66a, 69a, 70b; PPA 63b; Robert Ritchie 48b; Sandra Bit 143a; Saxon Holt 55a&b, 78a&b, 80a, 91, 98a&b, 116a, 120a&b, 135a&b; Therese D'Monte 149b.

This book is not intended as a "how-to" guide for eating garden plants. No plant or plant extract should be consumed unless you are certain of its identity and toxicity and of your potential for allergic reactions.

PC: P35

Table of Contents

We thank the following for their valuable time and beautiful images: All-America Selections, Brad Jalbert, Colin Laroque, Dawn Loewen, Debra Knapke, Don Doucette, Duncan Kelbaugh, Erika Flatt, Heather Markham, Karen Carriere, Laura Peters, Liz Klose, Peter Thompstone, the Perennial Plant Association, the Royal Botanic Gardens, Sandra Bit and all who allowed us to photograph their gardens.

Introduction

Starting a garden can seem like a daunting task. Which plants should you choose? Where should you put them in the garden? This book is intended to give beginner gardeners the information they need to start planning and planting gardens of their own. It describes a wide variety of plants and provides basic planting information such as where and how to plant.

California exhibits a diversity of ecological regions, each with its own unique challenges. Each region has a temperature range that indicates relative hardiness.

Consider this: 40° F is very different with consistent winter chill than without; in soggy soil or in dry; following a hot summer or a cold, wet one. These factors will have more influence on the survival of plants than will temperature. Recognizing the type of climate in which you garden will help you determine hardiness. Your local garden center should be able to provide you with local hardiness zones and frost date information.

Hardiness zones and frost dates are two terms often used when discussing climate. Hardiness zones consider the temperatures and conditions in winter. Plants are rated based on the zones in which they grow successfully. The last frost date in spring combined with the first frost date in fall helps us predict the length of the growing season.

Getting Started

When planning your garden, start with a quick analysis of the garden as it is now. Plants have different requirements, and it is best to put the right plant in the right place rather than to change your garden to suit the plants you want.

Knowing which parts of your garden receive the most and least amounts of sunlight will help you choose the proper plants and decide where to plant them. Light is classified into four basic groups: full sun (direct, unobstructed light for all or most of the day); partial shade (direct sun for about half the day and shade for the rest); light shade (shade for all or most of the day with some sun filtering through to ground level); and full shade (no direct sunlight). Most plants prefer a certain amount of light, but many can adapt to a range of light levels.

Plants use the soil to hold themselves upright and also rely on the many resources it holds: air, water, nutrients, organic matter and a host of microbes. The particle size of the soil influences the amount of air, water and nutrients it can hold. Sand, with the largest particles, has lots of air space and allows water and nutrients to drain quickly. Clay, with the smallest particles, is high in nutrients but has very little air space. Water is therefore slow to penetrate clay and slow to drain from it.

Soil acidity or alkalinity (measured on the pH scale) influences the nutrients available to plants. a pH of 7 is neutral; a lower pH is more acidic. Most plants prefer a soil with a pH of 5.5–7.5. Soil testing kits are available at most garden centers, and soil samples can be sent to testing facilities for a more thorough analysis.

Compost is one of the best and most important amendments you can add to any type of soil. Compost improves soil by adding organic matter and nutrients, introducing soil microbes, increasing water retention and improving drainage. Compost can be purchased, or you can make it in your own backyard.

Microclimates are small areas that are generally warmer or colder than the

Hardiness Zones Map

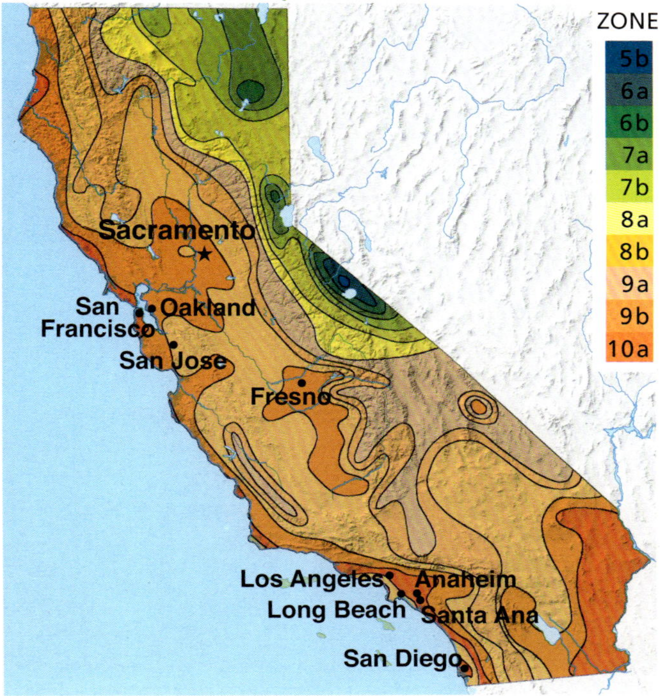

ZONE	TEMPERATURE (°F)
5b	−10 to −15
6a	−5 to −10
6b	0 to −5
7a	5 to 0
7b	10 to 5
8a	15 to 10
8b	20 to 15
9a	25 to 20
9b	30 to 25
10a	35 to 30

surrounding area. Buildings, fences, trees and other large structures can provide extra shelter in winter, but they may also trap heat in summer, creating a warmer microclimate. The bottoms of hills are usually colder than the tops, but may not be as windy. Take advantage of these areas when you plan your garden and choose your plants; you may even grow out-of-zone plants successfully in a warm, sheltered location.

Purchasing Plants

It's important to purchase healthy plants that are free of pests and diseases. Such plants will establish quickly in your garden and won't introduce problems that may spread to other plants. You should have a good idea of what the plant is supposed to look like—the color and shape of the leaves and the habit of the plant—and then inspect the plant for signs of disease or infestation.

The majority of plants are container grown. This method is an efficient way for nurseries and greenhouses to grow plants, but when plants grow in a restricted space for too long, they can become pot bound, with their roots densely encircling the inside of the pot. Avoid purchasing plants in this condition; they are often stressed and take longer to establish. Sometimes they may not establish at all. It is often possible to remove pots temporarily to look at the condition of the roots. Check for soil-borne insects and rotten roots at the same time.

Planting Basics

The following tips apply to all plants:

- Prepare the garden before planting. Dig over the soil, pull up any weeds and make any needed amendments before you begin planting, if possible. The prepared area should be at least twice the size of the plant you want to put in, and preferably the expected size of the mature plant. Consider using raised beds rather than planting directly in the ground to more easily control the type of soil, raise the level for easier access and provide easier digging and planting.
- Settle the soil with water. Good contact between the roots and the soil is important, but if you press the soil down too firmly, as often happens when you step on the soil, you can cause compaction, which reduces the movement of water through the soil and leaves very few air spaces. Instead, pour water in as you fill the hole with soil. The water will settle the soil evenly without allowing it to compact.
- Unwrap the roots. Remove any container before planting to give roots the chance to spread out naturally when planted. In particular, you should remove plastic containers, fiber pots, wire and burlap before planting trees. Fiber pots decompose very slowly, if at all, and wick moisture away from the plant. Synthetic burlap won't decompose, and wire can strangle the roots

1. Gently remove container.

2. Ensure proper planting depth.

3. Backfill with amended soil.

as they mature. The only exceptions to this rule are peat pots and pellets used to start annuals and vegetables; these decompose and can be planted with the young transplants. Bury the rim of the pot or pellet to avoid wicking moisture away.

- Accommodate the rootball. If you prepared your planting spot ahead of time, your planting hole will only need to be big enough to accommodate the rootball with the roots spread out slightly.
- Know the mature size. Plant based on how big the plants will grow rather than how big they are when you plant them. Large plants should have enough room to mature without interfering with walls, roof overhangs, power lines and walkways.
- Plant at the same depth. Plants generally like to grow at a certain level in relation to the soil and should be planted at the same level they were growing at before you transplanted them.
- Identify your plants. Keep track of what's what in your garden by putting a tag next to your plant when you plant it, or by making a drawing with plant names and locations. It is very easy for gardeners to forget exactly what they planted and where they planted it.
- Water deeply and infrequently. It's better to water deeply rather than to water a little bit more often. Infrequent watering forces roots to grow as they search for water and helps them survive dry spells when water bans may restrict your watering regime. Always check the rootzone by sticking your finger in the ground before you water, or use a moisture meter. More gardeners over water than under water.

Annuals and perennials in a mixed border

Choosing Plants

When choosing plants, aim for a variety of sizes, shapes, textures, features and bloom times. Features such as decorative fruit, variegated or colorful leaves and interesting bark provide something to look at when plants aren't blooming. This way you will have a garden that captivates your attention all year.

Annuals

Annuals are planted new each year and are expected to last only for a single growing season. Because of the long growing

4. Settle backfilled soil with water.

5. Water the plant well.

6. Add a layer of mulch.

season in parts of California, however, many annuals are grown as perennials. Their flowers and decorative foliage provide bright splashes of color and can fill in spaces around immature trees, shrubs and perennials.

Annuals are easy to plant and are usually sold in small packs of four or six. The roots quickly fill the space in these small packs, so the small rootball should be broken up before planting. Split the ball in two up the center or run your thumb up each side to break up the roots.

Many annuals are grown from seed and can be started directly in the garden. Consult an annuals book such as Lone Pine's *Annuals for Northern California* for further information on the care and growing of annuals.

Perennials

Perennials grow for three or more years. In colder regions, they may die back to the ground each fall and send up new shoots in spring. In warmer areas, many remain evergreen. They often have a shorter bloom period than annuals, but they usually require less care.

Trees and shrubs provide interest year-round.

Roses are lovely on their own or in mixed borders.

Many perennials benefit from being divided every few years. Dividing keeps them growing and blooming vigorously, and in some cases controls their spread. It involves digging the plant up, removing dead bits, breaking the plant into several pieces and then replanting some or all of the pieces. Extra pieces can be given as gifts to family, friends and neighbors.

Consult a perennials book such as Lone Pine's *Perennials for Northern California* for further information on the care of perennials.

Trees & Shrubs

Trees and shrubs provide the bones of the garden. Choose both carefully. In many parts of the state, trees and shrubs grow much taller and spread more enthusiastically than stated in the general descriptions. Characterized by leaf type, they may be deciduous or evergreen, and needled or broad-leaved.

Trees should have as little disturbed soil as possible at the bottom of the planting hole. Loose dirt settles over time, and sinking even an inch can kill some trees.

Staking is only necessary for newly planted trees over 5' tall. Pruning is more often required for shrubs than trees. It helps them maintain an attractive

Virginia creeper provides beautiful red fall color.

Lavender excels in sheltered, well-drained areas.

shape and can improve blooming. Consult Lone Pine's *Tree & Shrub Gardening for Northern California* for information about pruning trees and shrubs.

Roses

Roses are beautiful shrubs with lovely, often fragrant blooms. Traditionally, most roses only bloomed once in the growing season, but new varieties bloom all, or almost all, summer.

Generally, roses prefer a fertile, well-prepared planting area. a rule of thumb is to prepare an area 24" across, front to

Lilies bloom throughout the summer.

back and side to side, and 24" deep. Add plenty of compost or other fertile organic matter, and keep roses well watered during the growing season. Many roses are quite durable and will adapt to poorer conditions.

Roses, like all shrubs, have specific pruning requirements. a book such as Lone Pine's *Roses for Northern California* will provide detailed information.

Vines

Vines or climbing plants are useful for screening and shade, especially in a location too small for a tree. They may be woody or herbaceous and annual or perennial.

Most vines need sturdy supports to grow on. Trellises, arbors, porch railings, fences, walls, poles and trees are all possible supports. If a support is needed, ensure it's in place before you plant to avoid disturbing the roots later.

Bulbs

The bulb section of this book includes some plants that grow from corms and tubers. All of these plants have fleshy underground storage organs that allow them to survive extended periods of dormancy. They are often grown for the bright splashes of color their flowers provide. They may be spring, summer or fall flowering. Many bulbs require winter chill, so consider this when selecting your plantings.

Hardy bulbs can be left in the ground and will flower every year, but many popular tender plants grow from bulbs, corms or tubers and require a little more care.

Herbs

Herbs may be medicinal or culinary or both. a few common culinary herbs are listed in this book. Even if you don't cook with them, the often-fragrant foliage adds its aroma to the garden, and the plants have decorative forms, leaves and flowers.

Many herbs have pollen-producing flowers that attract butterflies, bees and hummingbirds to the garden. They also attract predatory insects. These useful insects help to manage your pest problems by feasting on insects such as aphids, mealy bugs and whiteflies.

Ornamental Grasses, Ferns and Other Foliage Plants

Foliage is an important consideration when choosing plants for your garden. Although many plants look spectacular in bloom, they can seem rather dull without flowers. Including a variety of plants with unique, interesting or striking foliage in your garden can provide all the color and texture you want without the need to rely on flowers.

Ornamental grasses add color, variety and texture.

Ornamental grasses are gaining popularity. Grasses offer a variety of textures and foliage colors, and at least three seasons of interest. Some grasses will thrive in any garden condition, including hot and dry to cool and wet temperatures, and in all types of soils.

Ornamental grasses have very few insect or disease problems. They require very little maintenance other than cutting the perennial grasses back in fall or spring. If you plan to leave dried grass standing for winter interest, be aware that it can present a fire hazard. Dry grass is highly flammable and should be cut back in fall if it is near a house or other structure.

Ferns are ancient plants that have adapted to many environments. The fern family is a very large group of plants with interesting foliage in a wide array of shapes and colors. Ferns do not produce flowers, but reproduce by spores borne in interesting structures on the undersides and margins of the foliage. Ferns are generally planted in moist, shaded areas of the garden, but some will thrive in dry shade under dense evergreens.

We included some grass-like foliage plants in this book. Sedge, rush and phormium can be used with or as substitutes for ornamental grasses. We also added a variety of plants grown for foliage throughout the book. Many annuals, perennials, trees, shrubs, vines and herbs have wonderful foliage and will be an asset to your garden landscape.

A Final Comment

Don't be afraid to experiment. No matter how many books you read, trying things yourself is the best way to learn and to find out what will grow in your garden. Use the information as guidelines, and have fun!

African Daisy

Osteospermum

African daisies are colorful, carefree plants that retain their good looks late into fall and can withstand temperatures as low as 25° F. New varieties have better heat and moisture tolerance.

Growing

Plant in **full sun**, in **light, evenly moist, moderately fertile, well-drained** soil when the soil warms in spring. Do not overwater or let the plants wilt; use organic mulch to cut down on watering. Deadhead to encourage new growth and more flowers. Pinch young plants to encourage a bushier form.

In temperate areas, African daisies behave like perennials. Just break off woody stalks, and the plants will regrow.

Tips

African daisies work well in containers or beds. Their flowers look great mixed with plants such as petunias and verbenas.

Recommended

O. ecklonis grows upright to almost prostrate, but it is often rejected in favor of its wonderful cultivars. **Passion Mix** has free-flowering, heat-tolerant plants. The **Springstar Series** boasts compact, early flowering plants. **Starwhirls Series** flowers have unique spoon-shaped petals.

O. fruticosum (trailing African daisy) is a carefree groundcover with purple and white flowers.

Proven Winners' ***O.* Symphony Series** has mounding plants. They tolerate heat well and flower throughout summer.

Also called: Cape daisy **Features:** colorful flowers; easy care; heat tolerance **Flower color:** white, peach, orange, yellow, pink, lavender, purple; often with dark centers of blue-purple or other colors **Height:** 12–20" **Spread:** 10–20"

Starwhirls Senes (above), *O. ecklonis* (below)

You may find African daisy listed as either Dimorphotheca *or* Osteospermum. Dimorphotheca *is a closely related genus that formerly included all the plants now listed as* Osteospermum.

Bachelor's Buttons

Centaurea

Bachelor's buttons are an old-time favorite, and they remain a popular and highly desirable annual today. In a garden with poor, rocky or sandy soil, pair these tough, hard-to-kill flowers with California poppies for a bright summer display.

Growing

Bachelor's buttons grow best in **full sun**. **Average to fertile, moist, well-drained** soil is preferable, but they will tolerate any soil, including poor and dry soil. Light frost won't harm the plants.

The long-lived cut flowers can be pinned to lapels or poked through buttonholes.

Seed started indoors should be planted in peat pots or pellets to avoid disturbing roots during transplanting. Plant out around the last frost. Shear spent flowers and old foliage in midsummer for fresh new growth. Deadhead to prolong blooming.

Tips

Bachelor's buttons are useful in a mixed border, wildflower bed or cottage-style garden. They look great when massed, work well in containers and make wonderful cut flowers.

Recommended

C. cyanus is an upright annual that self-seeds year after year. Many cultivars are available.

Also called: cornflower **Features:** bright flowers; tough, self-seeding plant **Flower color:** mostly blue; also shades of red, pink, white or purple **Height:** 8–32" **Spread:** 6–24"

Bacopa

Sutera

Bacopa snuggles under and around the stems of taller plants, forming a dense carpet dotted with tiny, white to pale lavender flowers, and eventually drifting over pot edges to form a cascade of stars.

Growing

Bacopa grows well in **full sun** or **partial shade**, with protection from the hot afternoon sun. The soil should be of **average fertility, humus rich, moist** and **well drained**.

If this plant dries out, its leaves will quickly die. Cut back dead growth to encourage new shoots to form.

Tips

Bacopa is a popular plant for hanging baskets, mixed containers and window boxes. It forms an attractive, spreading mound in a rock garden, but it will need regular watering. Mix it with million bells, geraniums, African daisies and many others.

Recommended

S. cordata is a compact, trailing plant that bears small, white flowers all summer. Cultivars with larger white flowers, lavender flowers or gold and green variegated foliage are available.

Bacopa is a perennial that is grown as an annual outdoors. It will thrive as a houseplant in a bright room.

Features: decorative flowers; foliage; habit
Flower color: white, lavender **Height:** 3–5"
Spread: 12–20"

Begonia

Begonia

B. × *tuberhybrida* (above & below)

Water along the edge of containers or around the dripline of in-ground tuberous begonias to prevent tuber rot—never water near the stem. Keep the mildew-prone foliage dry.

Whether you want beautiful flowers, a compact habit or decorative foliage, there is a begonia to fulfill your gardening needs. Once for shade gardens only, begonias now come in sun varieties as well.

Growing

Most begonias prefer **light to partial shade**, though some can also be planted in **full sun**. The soil should be **fertile, neutral to acidic** and **well-drained** with **lots of organic matter**. Some wax begonias tolerate sun if their soil is kept moist. Allow the soil to dry out slightly between waterings, particularly for tuberous begonias.

Plant begonias only in warm soil. In cold soil, they may become stunted and fail to thrive.

Tips

Plant trailing tuberous begonias in hanging baskets and along rock walls. Wax begonias make attractive edging plants. Rex begonias are useful as specimen plants in containers and beds.

Recommended

***B.* Rex Cultorum Hybrids** (rex begonias) are grown for their dramatic, colorful foliage.

B. semperflorens (wax begonias) have a neat, rounded habit, pink, white, red or bicolored flowers and green, bronze, reddish or white-variegated foliage. **'Buttered Popcorn'** from Proven Winners is a heat-tolerant begonia that can be planted in sun or shade.

B.* × *tuberhybrida (tuberous begonias) are generally sold as tubers. Their flowers bloom in many shades of red, pink, yellow, orange and white.

Features: colorful flowers; decorative foliage **Flower color:** white, pink, red, yellow, orange; bicolored or picotee **Height:** 6–24" **Spread:** 6–24"

Calendula

Calendula

'Apricot Surprise' (above), *C. officinalis* (below)

Calendulas are bright and charming. They produce attractive flowers in warm colors all summer and fall.

Growing

Calendula does equally well in **full sun** or **partial shade** in **well-drained** soil of **average fertility**. It likes cool weather and can withstand a light frost. Deadhead to prolong blooming and to keep plants looking neat.

Young plants are sometimes difficult to find in nurseries. Sow seed directly into the garden in mid-spring. A second sowing in early summer ensures a good fall display.

Tips

This informal plant looks attractive in borders and mixed into the vegetable garden. It can also be used in mixed planters.

Also called: pot marigold, English marigold
Features: colorful flowers; long blooming period
Flower color: cream, yellow, gold, orange, apricot **Height:** 12–30" **Spread:** 12–18"

Recommended

C. officinalis is a vigorous, tough, upright plant that bears daisy-like, single or double flowers in a wide range of yellow and orange shades. Several cultivars are available.

Calendula flowers can be added to stews for color or to salads for flavor. They can also be brewed into an infusion that is useful as a wash for minor cuts and bruises.

California Poppy

Eschscholzia

California poppies cheerfully reseed themselves year after year. They look great in meadow or rock gardens, or popping up through cracks of a flagstone path.

Growing

California poppy prefers **full sun** and **well-drained** soil of **poor to average fertility**. In rich soil, the plant will grow lush and green but will bear few, if any, flowers. This plant is drought tolerant once established, but it requires a lot of water for germination and until it begins flowering.

Never start this plant indoors because it dislikes having its roots disturbed.

California poppy will sprout quickly when sown directly in the garden in early to mid-spring. In mild areas, seeds sown in early fall will produce blooms in spring.

Tips

California poppies can be included in an annual border or annual planting in a cottage garden.

Recommended

E. californica forms a mound of delicate, feathery, blue-green foliage. It bears satiny flowers all summer. Cultivars with semi-double or double flowers and flowers in red, cream or pink are available.

The petals of California poppy are edible. They have little nutritional value, but the color will brighten up a salad.

Features: colorful flowers; attractive, feathery foliage **Flower color:** orange, yellow, red; less commonly pink, violet or cream **Height:** 12–24" **Spread:** 6–12"

China Aster

Callistephus

China aster's vivid, dense flowers will steal the spotlight in your garden all summer long—provided you feed and water it adequately.

Growing

China aster prefers **full sun** but tolerates partial shade. The soil should be **neutral to alkaline, fertile, evenly moist** and **well drained**. If your garden has acidic soil, grow smaller China aster varieties in pots or planters, where the soil pH can be adjusted.

Plant out once the soil has warmed. This plant doesn't like having its roots disturbed, so start seeds in peat pots or peat pellets. China aster has a shallow root system that can dry out quickly; mulch to conserve moisture.

Tips

Use smaller varieties as edging and taller varieties for cut flowers and at the back of the border. Tall varieties may require staking.

Recommended

C. chinensis is the source of many varieties and cultivars, which come in three height groups: dwarf, medium and tall.

China asters are heavy feeders, so you will need to fertilize them regularly to produce flowers like those in the catalogs.

Features: colorful flowers of varying shapes and sizes **Flower color:** purple, blue, pink, red, white, peach, yellow **Height:** 12–36" **Spread:** 10–18"

Coleus

Solenostemon (Coleus)

Coleus has almost limitless colors, textures and variations. Exciting new varieties for sun extend this dramatic, colorful plant beyond the shade garden.

Growing

Coleus grows best in **partial shade** or **full sun** depending on the variety. The soil should be **average to fertile, humus rich, moist** and **well drained**. Pinch off flower buds once they have developed. Coleus flowers tend to stretch out and become less attractive after they bloom. Pinching encourages bushiness.

Place the seeds in a refrigerator for one or two days before planting them on the soil surface; the cold temperatures help the seeds break dormancy. They need light to germinate. Seedlings will be green at first, but leaf variegation will develop as the plants mature.

Tips

Coleus looks dramatic grouped in beds, borders and mixed containers, or planted as edging.

Recommended

S. scutellarioides (*Coleus blumei* var. *verschaffeltii*) forms a bushy mound of multi-colored, slightly toothed to very ruffled foliage. Dozens of cultivars are available, but many cannot be started from seed. Some interesting cultivars include the lime green **'Wasabi'** and the beautifully vibrant **Kong Series**.

Features: brightly colored foliage **Flower color:** light purple; grown as a foliage plant **Height:** 6–36" **Spread:** usually equal to height

Try taking coleus cuttings from a mother plant and overwintering them inside. The cuttings root easily in a glass of water.

Cosmos

Cosmos

C. bipinnatus (above & below)

Cosmos are low-cost, low-maintenance cottage garden flowers that are easy to grow and never fail to delight.

Growing

Cosmos like **full sun** and **well-drained** soil of **poor to average fertility**. Plant them after the last frost. Overfertilizing and overwatering can reduce the number of flowers; cut faded blooms to encourage more buds. These plants often self-seed.

Tips

Cosmos look attractive in cottage gardens, at the back of a border or mass planted in an informal bed.

To stake plants, push twiggy branches into the ground when the plants are young. Cosmos will grow up between the branches, and the mature plant will hide the branches. To avoid staking, plant cosmos against a fence or in a sheltered location, or grow its shorter varieties.

Recommended

C. bipinnatus (annual cosmos) is an erect plant with fine, fern-like foliage. It and its many cultivars bear magenta, rose, pink, white or bicolored flowers, usually with yellow centers.

C. sulphureus (yellow cosmos) is smaller and denser than *C. bipinnatus* and has gold, orange, scarlet or yellow flowers. Sow this plant directly in the garden.

The genus name Cosmos *is from the Greek* kosmos, *meaning "good order" or "harmony."*

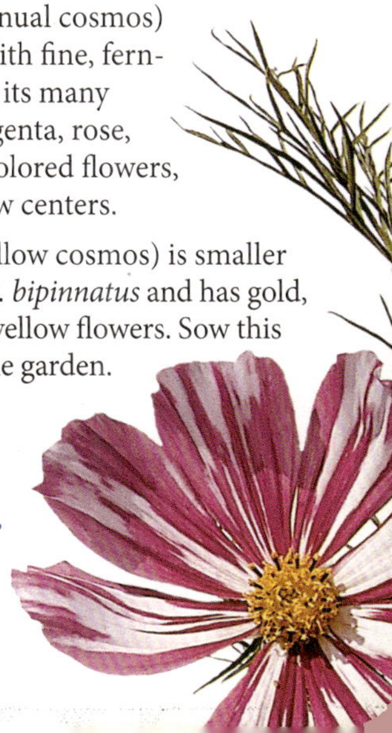

Features: colorful flowers; fern-like foliage; easy to grow **Flower color:** magenta, rose, pink, purple, white, yellow, orange, scarlet **Height:** 12"–7' **Spread:** 12–18"

Dusty Miller

Senecio

Dusty miller makes an artful addition to planters, window boxes and mixed borders where the soft, silvery gray, deeply lobed foliage makes a good backdrop for the brightly colored flowers of other annuals.

Growing

Dusty miller prefers **full sun** but tolerates light shade. The soil should be of **average fertility** and **well drained**. Pinch off the flowers before they bloom. They aren't showy, and they steal energy that would otherwise go to producing more foliage.

Dusty miller will overwinter in mild areas near the coast. Don't prune it until March, and then cut back the winter-weary foliage almost to the ground. By June, the plants will be fresh with new growth.

Mix dusty miller with geraniums, begonias or cockscombs to bring out the vibrant colors of those flowers.

Tips

This plant's soft, silvery, lacy foliage is its main feature. Dusty miller is used primarily as an edging plant, but also in beds, borders and containers.

Recommended

S. cineraria forms a mound of fuzzy, silvery gray, lobed or finely divided foliage. Many cultivars with impressive foliage colors and shapes have been developed.

Features: silvery foliage; neat habit **Flower color:** yellow to cream; grown as a foliage plant **Height:** 12–24" **Spread:** equal to or slightly narrower than height

Dwarf Morning Glory

Convolvulus

This well-mannered, relatively pest-free plant is easy to care for. It's a great addition to a new garden because it doesn't need fertile or well-worked soil, and it adapts to poor growing conditions.

Growing

Dwarf morning glories prefer **full sun**. The soil should be of **poor to average fertility** and **well drained**. These plants may not flower well in rich, moist soil.

Sow seeds or plant in mid- to late spring. Soak the seeds in water overnight before sowing them. If starting seeds early indoors, use peat pots to avoid root damage when transplanting.

Tips

Plant these compact, mounding plants in containers, hanging baskets, rock walls and borders.

Recommended

C. tricolor bears flowers that last only a single day, blooming in the morning and twisting shut that evening. Several cultivars are available.

*This annual is related to the dreaded bindweeds (*C. arvensis *and* C. sepium*), but it doesn't share its weedy cousins' unstoppable twining and spreading power.*

Features: richly colored flowers; easy care **Flower color:** blue, purple, pink **Height:** 12–16" **Spread:** 9–12"

Fan Flower

Scaevola

Fan flower's intriguing one-sided flowers add interest to hanging baskets, planters and window boxes.

Growing

Fan flower grows well in **full sun** or **light shade**. The soil should be of **average fertility, moist** and very **well drained**. Water regularly because this plant doesn't like to dry out completely. It does, however, recover quickly from wilting when watered.

Fan flower responds well to pinching and trimming. Frequently pinching the tips or trimming the entire plant back will keep it bushy and blooming.

Tips

Fan flower is a popular choice for hanging baskets and containers, but it can also be used along the tops of rock walls and in rock gardens, where it will trail down. In mixed borders it can be planted under shrubs, where it will form an attractive groundcover.

Recommended

S. aemula forms a mound of foliage from which trailing stems emerge. The fan-shaped flowers come in shades of purple, usually with white bases. The species is rarely grown because there are many improved cultivars. **'Blue Wonder'** has long, trailing branches. **'Saphira'** is compact with deep blue flowers.

Given the right conditions, this Australian plant will flower profusely from April through to frost.

Features: unique flowers; trailing habit **Flower color:** blue, purple **Height:** up to 8" **Spread:** up to 4'

Fuchsia

Fuchsia

These beautiful, shade-blooming plants should be grown in every garden. Once the province of cool-summer areas, fuchsias are now available in heat-tolerant varieties.

F. × *hybrida* (above & below)

Growing

Fuchsias prefer **partial** or **light shade**; full sun can be too hot for them. The soil should be **fertile, moist** and **well drained**. Plant them after the last frost.

Deadhead fuchsias by plucking the swollen seedpods from behind the fading petals, or the seeds will ripen and rob the plant of the energy it needs for flower production. Fuchsias bloom on new growth and prefer a plant food high in nitrogen.

Tips

Plant upright fuchsias in mixed planters, beds and borders. Pendulous fuchsias are most often used in hanging baskets, but they make attractive additions to planters and rock gardens.

Recommended

***F.* Angel Earrings Series** from Proven Winners tolerate heat and humidity.

Dozens of cultivars of ***F.* × *hybrida*** are available in both upright and pendulous forms. Cultivars with bronzy red foliage are also available. The **California Dreamers Series** has heat-tolerant varieties with large blooms in a variety of colors.

Some gardeners who have grown hardy fuchsias over several years have trained the plants to adopt tree forms.

Features: colorful, pendant flowers **Flower color:** pink, red, orange, purple, purple-blue, white; often bicolored **Height:** 6–36" **Spread:** 8–36"

Gazania

Gazania

Cheerful, daisy-like flowers and a spreading habit make gazania a reliable groundcover. The flowers open on sunny days and close in the evenings and on cloudy days.

Growing

Gazanias prefer **full sun** or **partial shade** in **poor to average, sandy, well-drained** soil. Although they do best with regular water, they tolerate infrequent irrigation once established. Deadhead for repeat blooms.

This native of southern Africa has very few pests or problems and transplants easily, even when blooming.

Tips

Place gazanias between slow-growing perennials to provide a burst of color. Because they require minimal care, gazanias are useful in parking strips or other areas that are difficult to irrigate on a regular basis.

Recommended

***G.* hybrids** are available in clumping and spreading varieties. Colors include cream, yellow, orange, pink and red. Some feature stripes and contrasting colors.

Although it is usually grown as an annual, gazania is a perennial that may survive winter in the warmer areas of California.

Also called: treasure flower **Features:** low, spreading foliage; daisy-like flowers **Flower color:** red, orange, yellow, pink, cream **Height:** usually 6–8"; may reach 12–18" **Spread:** 8–12"

Geranium

Pelargonium

Tough, predictable, sun-loving and drought-resistant, geraniums have earned their respected place in the annual garden. For something out of the ordinary, seek out the scented geraniums with their fragrant and often decorative foliage.

Growing

Geraniums prefer **full sun** but tolerate partial shade, though they may not bloom as profusely. The soil should be **fertile** and **well drained**.

Deadheading is essential to keep geraniums blooming and looking neat. In zones 9–11, treat geraniums as perennials.

Tips

Geraniums are used in borders, beds, planters, hanging baskets and window boxes.

Recommended

P. domesticum (Martha Washington geranium) has heart-shaped foliage and larger, frillier flowers than other geraniums. It works well in containers but does not tolerate heat as well as do other varieties.

P. peltatum (ivy-leaved geranium) has thick, waxy leaves and a trailing habit. Ivy-leaved geranium is one of the best plants to include in a mixed hanging basket.

P. zonale (zonal geranium) is a bushy plant with red, pink, purple, orange or white flowers and, frequently, banded or multi-colored foliage.

P. zonale (above), *P. domesticum* (below)

Some ***P.*** **species** and **cultivars** have scented foliage. The scents are grouped into the categories of rose, mint, citrus, fruit, spice and pungent.

Features: colorful flowers; decorative or scented foliage; variable habits **Flower color:** red, pink, violet, orange, salmon, white, purple **Height:** 8–24" **Spread:** 6"–4'

Impatiens

Impatiens

I. hawkeri (above & below)

Impatiens are the high-wattage darlings of the shade garden, delivering masses of colorful flowers.

Growing

Impatiens do best in **partial shade** or **light shade** but tolerate full shade or, if kept moist, full sun. New Guinea and balsam impatiens grow well in sunny locations. The soil should be **fertile, humus rich, moist** and **well drained**.

Busy Lizzie is so named because it flowers continuously throughout the growing season.

Tips

Impatiens are known for their ability to grow and flower profusely even in shade. Mass plant them in beds under trees, along shady fences or walls or in porch planters. They look lovely in hanging baskets.

Recommended

I. balsamina (balsam impatiens) are upright plants that bloom in shades of purple, red, pink or white. Several double-flowered cultivars exist.

I. hawkeri (New Guinea hybrids; New Guinea impatiens) flowers in shades of red, orange, pink, purple or white. The foliage is often variegated with a yellow stripe down the center of each leaf.

I. walleriana (busy Lizzie) flowers in shades of purple, red, burgundy, pink, yellow, salmon, orange, apricot or white, or it can be bicolored. Dozens of cultivars are available.

Features: colorful flowers; grows well in shade
Flower color: shades of purple, red, burgundy, pink, yellow, salmon, orange, apricot, white; also bicolored
Height: 6–36" **Spread:** 12–24"

Licorice Plant

Helichrysum

'Silver' (above), 'Limelight' (below)

This tough plant can handle frosty weather, rain storms, heat waves, browsing deer and pesky slugs. It's a perfect choice for carefree gardeners.

Growing

Licorice plant prefers **full sun**. The soil should be of **poor to average fertility, neutral to alkaline** and **well drained**. Licorice plant wilts when the soil dries but revives quickly once watered. If it outgrows its space, snip it back with a pair of pruners, shears or even scissors.

Tips

Licorice plant is a perennial grown as an annual, and it is prized for its foliage rather than its flowers. Include it in your hanging baskets, planters and window boxes to provide a soft, silvery backdrop to the colorful flowers of other plants. Licorice plant can also be used as a groundcover in beds, borders, rock gardens and along the tops of retaining walls.

Features: trailing habit; colorful, fuzzy foliage
Flower color: grown as a foliage plant
Height: 20" **Spread:** about 36"; sometimes up to 6'

Recommended

H. petiolare is a trailing plant with fuzzy, gray-green leaves. Cultivars are more common than the species and include varieties with lime green, silver or variegated leaves.

Licorice plant is a good indicator plant for hanging baskets. When you see licorice plant wilting, it is time to water.

Lobelia

Lobelia

'Sapphire' (above), Cascade Series (below)

Lobelia is a lovely plant that adds color to shady spots and blends well with fuchsias and begonias. Lobelia also does well in the sun and makes a striking combination with marigolds.

Growing

Lobelia grows well in **full sun** or **partial shade**, in **fertile, moist, well-drained** soil high in **organic matter**. Lobelia likes cool summer nights. In hot areas, it may die back over summer but usually revives as the weather cools. To keep it blooming through summer, ensure that its soil stays moist in hot weather and trim the plant back after its first wave of flowers.

Because seedlings are prone to damping off, be sure to use good, clean, seed-starting soil mix. Damping off causes plants to rot at the soil level, flop over and die.

These lovely plants from the bellflower family contain deadly alkaloids and have poisoned people who tried to use them as herbal medicine.

Tips

Use lobelia along the edges of beds and borders, on rock walls or in rock gardens, mixed containers and hanging baskets.

Recommended

L. erinus may be rounded and bushy or low and trailing. Many cultivars are available in both forms. **Laguna Series** has heat resistant, trailing plants in a variety of colors. **Riviera Series** features compact, bushy plants.

Features: abundant, colorful flowers **Flower color:** purple, blue, pink, white, red **Height:** 3–9" **Spread:** 6" or more

Mallow

Lavatera

L. trimestris (above), *L. cachemiriana* (below)

Mallow is great for tough growing conditions. Many plants fail in dry, infertile soil, but mallow just keeps blooming.

Growing

Mallow prefers **full sun**. The soil should be of **average fertility, light** and **well drained**. This plant likes cool, moist weather and shelter from the wind. Stake tall varieties to keep them from falling over.

Use peat pots when starting seeds indoors. Mallow resents having its roots disturbed. Direct seeding is best. Plant out in spring.

Tips

These large, shrubby plants work well in beds and borders or behind smaller plants for a colorful backdrop. Or try planting them as a temporary hedge. The flowers can be used for cutting and are edible.

Features: delicate flowers; tough plant; easy care **Flower color:** rose, pink, salmon, white **Height:** 24"–4' **Spread:** 18–24"

Recommended

L. arborea (tree mallow) is a large plant with funnel-shaped, pinkish purple flowers.

L. cachemiriana is another large plant that bears light pink flowers.

L. trimestris is a bushy plant that bears red, pink, rose pink, salmon pink or white, funnel-shaped flowers.

Although only 25 species of Lavatera *exist, it is a diverse group of annuals, biennials, perennials and shrubs.*

Marigold

Tagetes

T. patula (above & below)

From the large, exotic, ruffled flowers of African marigold to the tiny flowers on the low-growing signet marigold, the warm colors and fresh scent of marigolds add a festive air to the garden.

Growing

Marigolds grow best in **full sun**. The soil should be of **average fertility** and **well drained**. These plants are drought tolerant and hold up well in windy, rainy weather. However, too much water may cause rot. Minimize overhead watering.

Sow seed directly in the garden after the chance of frost has passed. Deadhead to prolong blooming and to keep plants tidy.

Tips

Mass planted or mixed with other plants, marigolds make a vibrant addition to beds, borders and container gardens. These plants will thrive in the hottest, driest parts of your garden.

Slugs really enjoy marigolds' scented foliage—be sure to protect your plants from these creatures.

Recommended

T. erecta (African marigold, American marigold, Aztec marigold) is the largest plant with the biggest flowers.

T. patula (French marigold) is low growing and has a wide range of flower colors.

T. tenuifolia (signet marigold) has feathery foliage and small, dainty flowers.

***T.* Triploid Hybrids** have huge flowers and compact growth.

Features: brightly colored flowers; fragrant foliage; easy to grow **Flower color:** yellow, red, orange, brown, gold, cream; also bicolored **Height:** 6–36" **Spread:** 12–24"

Million Bells

Calibrachoa

Million bells are charming and, given the right conditions, will bloom continually throughout the growing season.

Growing

Million bells prefer **full sun**. The soil should be **fertile, moist** and **well drained**. Although they prefer to be watered regularly, million bells are fairly drought resistant once established. The flowers develop hardiness as the weather cools, enabling them to bloom well into autumn. Million bells can survive overnight temperatures as low as 20° F.

They grow all summer and fall and need plenty of room to spread, or they will overtake other flowers. Pinch back to keep plants compact. If they get scraggly, trim back by one-third.

Tips

A popular choice for planters and hanging baskets, million bells also look attractive in beds and borders. To protect the flower petals from rain, place hanging baskets under the eaves of the house or porch.

Recommended

C. hybrids have a dense, trailing habit, and they bear small flowers that look like petunias. Cultivars are available in a wide range of flower colors, including striking bicolored varieties. The peachy **'Terracotta'** looks great paired with intensely colored foliage plants in clay pots.

Also called: calibrachoa, trailing petunia
Features: colorful flowers; trailing habit
Flower color: pink, purple, yellow, red-orange, white, blue **Height:** 6–12" **Spread:** up to 24"

'Trailing Blue' (above), 'Trailing Pink' (below)

The flowers of million bells close at night and on cloudy days.

Moss Rose

Portulaca

For a brilliant show in the hottest, driest, most neglected area of the garden, you can't go wrong with moss rose.

Growing

Moss rose requires **full sun**. The soil should be of **poor fertility, sandy** and **well drained**. As long as the location is sunny, this plant will do well with minimal care, but remember to water it occasionally.

To ensure that you will have plants where you want them, start seed indoors. If you sow directly outdoors, the tiny seeds may get washed away by rain, and the plants will pop up in unexpected places.

Tips

Moss rose will grow well under the eaves of a house or in a dry, rocky, exposed area. It also makes a great addition to a hanging basket on a sunny front porch.

Place these plants close together and allow them to intertwine for an interesting and attractive effect.

Recommended

P. grandiflora forms a bushy mound of succulent foliage. It bears delicate, papery, rose-like flowers profusely all summer and fall. Many cultivars are available, including some with flowers that stay open on cloudy days.

Also called: portulaca **Features:** colorful, drought-resistant summer flowers **Flower color:** red, pink, yellow, white, purple, orange, peach **Height:** 4–8" **Spread:** 6–12" or more

Nasturtium

Tropaeolum

These fast-growing, brightly colored flowers are popular with beginners and experienced gardeners alike.

'Alaska' (above), *T. majus* (below)

Growing

Nasturtiums prefer **full sun** but tolerate some shade. The soil should be of **poor to average fertility, light, moist** and **well drained**. Plants grown in fertile soil will produce many leaves but few flowers. Let the soil drain completely between waterings.

Set out plants or sow directly in the garden in spring and fall.

Tips

Nasturtiums are used in beds, borders, containers and hanging baskets. The climbing varieties are grown up trellises or over rock walls or places that need concealing. Trailing variegated leaf varieties are particularly striking in hanging baskets.

These plants thrive in poor locations, and they make an interesting addition to hard-to-mow slopes.

Recommended

T. majus has a trailing habit, but many of the cultivars have bushier, more refined habits. Cultivars are available in a range of flower colors and with variegated foliage. **Alaska Mix** features striped leaves in a mounding plant with bright flowers.

Combine nasturtiums with vegetables and other ornamental edible plants in containers and window boxes. The leaves and flowers add a peppery flavor to salads.

Features: brightly colored flowers; attractive leaves; edible leaves and flowers; varied habits **Flower color:** red, orange, yellow, burgundy, pink, cream, gold, white; also bicolored **Height:** 12–18" for dwarf varieties; up to 10' for trailing varieties **Spread:** equal to height

Petunia

Petunia

'Blue Wave' (above), multiflora petunias (above & below)

For speedy growth, prolific blooming and ease of care, petunias are hard to beat. Even the most neglected plants will continue to bloom all summer.

Growing

Petunias prefer **full sun**. The soil should be of **average fertility, light, sandy** and **well drained**. In midsummer, pinch the plant back halfway or cut the blooms for arrangements. This will keep the plant compact and bushy and will encourage new growth and flowers.

When sowing, press seeds into soil surface, but don't cover them with soil.

The huge selection of petunias ensures that there is one for every garden.

Tips

Use petunias in beds, borders, containers and hanging baskets.

Recommended

P.* × *hybrida is a large group of popular annuals that fall into three categories: **grandifloras** have the largest flowers in the widest range of colors; **multifloras** bear more but smaller flowers; **millifloras** have the smallest flowers in the narrowest range of colors, but they are the most prolific bloomers. Some varieties are very fragrant.

***P.* Storm Series** are grandiflora petunias that are weather and disease tolerant and bear large blooms in a range of colors.

***P.* Wave Series** are vigorous, spreading plants tolerant of rain and cold that bloom almost nonstop.

Features: colorful flowers; versatile plants **Flower color:** pink, purple, red, white, yellow, coral, blue; also bicolored **Height:** 6–18" **Spread:** 12–24" or more

Salvia

Salvia

Salvias should have a place in every annual garden. There are over 900 species of Salvia, and the attractive and varied forms have something to offer every garden style.

Growing

Salvias prefer **full sun** but will tolerate light shade. The soil should be **moist, well drained** and of **average to rich fertility** with lots of **organic matter** mixed in. To keep plants producing flowers, water often and fertilize monthly.

Tips

Salvias look good grouped in beds and borders and in containers. The long-lasting cut flowers are good for arrangements.

Recommended

S. coccinea (Texas sage) is a bushy, upright plant that bears whorled spikes of white, pink, blue or purple flowers.

S. farinacea (mealy cup sage, blue sage) has bright blue flowers clustered along stems powdered with silver. Cultivars are available.

S. greggi (autumn sage) is a compact, shrubby perennial that does well in southern California.

S. splendens (salvia, scarlet sage) is grown for its spikes of bright red, tubular flowers. Recently, cultivars have become available in white, pink, purple or orange.

S. viridis (*S. horminium*; annual clary sage) is grown for its colorful pink, purple, blue or white bracts, not its flowers.

S. splendens (above), *S. farinacea* (below)

The genus name Salvia *comes from the Latin* salvus, *meaning "save," referring to the medicinal properties of several species.*

Also called: sage **Features:** colorful summer flowers; attractive foliage **Flower color:** red, blue, purple, burgundy, pink, orange, salmon, yellow, cream, white; also bicolored **Height:** 8–36" **Spread:** 8–16"

Snapdragon

Antirrhinum

Snapdragons are among the most appealing plants. The flower colors are always rich and vibrant, and even the most jaded gardeners are tempted to squeeze open the dragons' mouths.

Growing

Snapdragons prefer **full sun** but tolerate light or partial shade. The soil should be **fertile, rich in organic matter, neutral to alkaline** and **well drained**. These plants do not perform well in acidic soil.

Do not cover seeds when sowing because they require light for germination.

Snapdragons may survive winter, but they grow best when they're planted annually.

To encourage bushy growth, pinch the tips of the young plants. Cut off the flower spikes as they fade to promote further blooming and to prevent the plant from dying back before the end of the season.

Tips

The height of the variety dictates the best place for it in a border—the shortest varieties work well near the front, and the tallest look good in the back. The dwarf and medium-height varieties can be used in planters. Trailing varieties do well in hanging baskets.

Recommended

There are many cultivars of ***A. majus*** available, generally grouped into three size categories: dwarf, medium and giant.

Features: entertaining, colorful summer flowers **Flower color:** white, cream, yellow, orange, red, maroon, pink, purple; also bicolored **Height:** 6"–4' **Spread:** 6–24"

Sunflower

Helianthus

The image of sunflowers against a weathered barn or tall garden fence has inspired artists of all ages throughout history.

'Teddy Bear' (above), *H. annuus* (below)

Growing

Sunflowers grow best in **full sun**. The soil should be of **average fertility, humus rich, moist** and **well drained**.

The annual sunflower is an excellent plant for children to grow. The seeds are big and easy to handle, and they germinate quickly. The plant's upward growth can be measured until the flower blooms on top.

Tips

The lower-growing varieties can be used in beds and borders. The tall varieties are effective at the back of borders and make good screens and temporary hedges. The tallest varieties may need staking.

Carefree gardeners let sunflowers go to seed in the garden to produce new blooms the following summer.

Recommended

H. annuus is considered weedy, but it has produced many attractive new cultivars.

Birds will flock to the ripening seedheads of your sunflowers and quickly pluck out the tightly packed seeds.

Features: late summer flowers; edible seeds **Flower color:** most commonly yellow, but also orange, red, brown or cream, or bicolored; typically brown, purple or rusty red centers **Height:** dwarf varieties, 24"; giants up to 15' **Spread:** 12–24"

Sweet Alyssum

Lobularia

Sweet alyssum makes a lovely carpet of blooms to weave through formal and informal plantings. It is excellent for creating soft edges in beds, borders, containers and along pathways.

Growing

Sweet alyssum prefers **full sun** but tolerates light shade. **Well-drained** soil of **average fertility** is preferred, but poor soil is tolerated. Once established, it readily reseeds.

Sweet alyssum may die back a bit during hot, humid summers. Trim it back and water it periodically to encourage new growth and more flowers when the weather cools.

Tips

Sweet alyssum creeps around rock gardens, over rock walls and along the edges of beds. It is an excellent choice for seeding into cracks and crevices of walkways and between patio stones. It is also good for filling spaces between taller plants in borders and mixed containers.

Recommended

L. maritima forms a low, spreading mound of foliage. The entire plant appears to be covered in tiny blossoms when in full flower. Cultivars are available in a wide range of flower colors.

Leave alyssum plants out all winter. In spring, remove the previous year's growth to expose the self-sown seedlings below.

Features: fragrant flowers **Flower color:** pink, purple, yellow, salmon, white **Height:** 3–12" **Spread:** 6–24"

Sweet Potato Vine

Ipomoea

'Margarita' (above), 'Terrace Lime' (below)

This vigorous, rambling plant has lime green, bruised purple or green, pink and cream variegated leaves, and it can make any gardener look like a genius.

Growing

Grow sweet potato vine in **full sun**. Any type of soil will do, but a **light**, **well-drained** soil of **poor fertility** is preferred.

Tips

Sweet potato vine is a great addition to mixed planters, window boxes and hanging baskets. It will scramble around a rock garden and cascade over the edge of a retaining wall. These cascading plants can also be trained to grow up a trellis.

As a bonus, when you pull up your plant at the end of summer, you can eat any tubers (sweet potatoes) that have formed.

Features: decorative foliage **Flower color:** grown as a foliage plant **Height:** about 12" **Spread:** up to 15' for the species; cultivars, 4–6'

Recommended

I. batatas is best recognized by its large, lime green, heart-shaped leaves. Cultivars are available in shades of purple and with different leaf shapes. A variety with tri-colored foliage is also available. Unlike the more aggressive members of the family, this species has a very civilized look. It drapes neatly over the sides of containers and spreads over the soil beneath taller plants.

Verbena

Verbena

V. canadensis (above), *V.* × *hybrida* (below)

This annual demands dry, well-drained soil, so it is best grown on sunny mounds, along raised median strips and with plants that suck moisture out of the soil, such as junipers.

Growing

Verbenas grow best in **full sun**. The soil should be **fertile** and very **well drained**. Pinch back young plants for bushy growth. Cut plants back by half in midsummer to encourage lots of fall blooms.

Verbena's form and range of colors make it an ideal addition to hanging baskets. Just group it with other plants that need well-drained, dry soil, such as bacopa and lantana.

Tips

Use verbenas on rock walls and in beds, borders, rock gardens, containers, hanging baskets and window boxes. They make good substitutes for ivy-leaved geraniums where the sun is hot and where a roof overhang keeps the mildew-prone verbenas dry.

Recommended

V. bonariensis forms a low clump of foliage from which tall, stiff stems bear clusters of small, purple flowers.

***V. canadensis* 'Homestead Purple'** is a very vigorous plant that may come back the following spring in mild winter areas.

V.* × *hybrida is a bushy plant that may be upright or spreading. It bears clusters of small flowers in a wide range of colors. Cultivars are available.

Also called: garden verbena **Features:** summer and fall flowers **Flower color:** red, pink, purple, blue, yellow, scarlet, silver, peach, white; some with white centers **Height:** 8"–5' **Spread:** 12–36"

Viola

Viola

V. × *wittrockiana* (above), *V. tricolor* (below)

Viola is a cottage garden staple. Two of its most popular species—pansies and Johnny-jump-ups—reseed and create a dazzling display in odd places such as gravel driveways, between evergreen shrubs and in sidewalk cracks.

Growing

Violas prefer **full sun** but tolerate partial shade. The soil should be **fertile, moist** and **well drained**.

Violas do best when the weather is cool, and they may die back completely in hot summers. Plants may rejuvenate in fall, but it is often easier to plant new ones to ensure your garden looks its best.

Tips

Violas can be used in beds, borders and containers, and they look great mixed in with spring-flowering bulbs.

Recommended

V. tricolor (Johnny-jump-up) is a popular species. The flowers are purple, white and yellow, usually in combination, though several varieties have flowers in a single color, often purple.

V.* × *wittrockiana (pansy) comes in blue, purple, red, orange, yellow, pink or white, often multi-colored or with face-like markings. Many cultivars are available.

Sow seeds indoors in early winter for spring flowers and in midsummer for fall and early winter blooms. More seeds will germinate if they are kept in darkness until they sprout.

Features: colorful flowers; easy to grow **Flower color:** blue, purple, red, orange, yellow, pink, white; also multi-colored **Height:** 3–10" **Spread:** 6–12"

Zinnia

Zinnia

Cheerful zinnias are sturdy plants that mix well with other annuals and can also hold their own in the vegetable garden as a decorative accent.

Growing

Zinnias favor hot weather and **full sun**. The soil should be **fertile, moist** and **well drained**. Some varieties are prone to mildew, so play it safe and limit overhead watering.

The plants are easy to grow from seed. Deadhead to prolong blooming and to keep plants looking neat.

Tips

Zinnias are available in tall, medium and dwarf varieties. If you have a border, plant tall varieties in back and dwarf versions in front for a colorful display.

Recommended

Z. elegans is available in a variety of cultivars including **'Envy,'** a 36" tall version with lime green flowers, and **'Dahlia Flowered Mix,'** with 4–5" wide, double blooms.

Mildew can be a problem for zinnias, so choose mildew-resistant cultivars and grow them in locations with good air circulation.

Features: bushy plants; colorful flowers **Flower color:** red, yellow, green, purple, orange, pink, white, maroon, brown, gold; often bicolored or tricolored **Height:** 6–36" **Spread:** 12–24"

Agapanthus

Agapanthus

Even when not in bloom, agapanthus contributes clumps of bright green foliage to the garden, providing a lush background for companions with lots of flowers but sparse foliage or for taller plants with leggy lower limbs.

Growing

Agapanthus grows well in **full sun, partial shade** or **light shade**. Provide protection from the hottest afternoon sun. Soil should be **moist** and **well drained**. These hardy plants withstand temperature fluctuations and stay evergreen to about 25° F.

Tips

Agapanthus makes an excellent filler plant. The strap-like leaves are bright green, and the rounded or pendulous clusters of flowers atop long, straight stems make excellent companions to flowering shrubs and large shrub-like perennials.

Recommended

A. orientalis is evergreen and sports broad, arching leaves in big clumps. It is the most commonly planted. Many hybrids and cultivars are available. **'Ellamae'** and **'Storm Cloud'** have bright blue flowers. White varieties include **'Queen Anne'** and **'Rancho White.' 'Peter Pan'** is a popular dwarf variety.

Agapanthus is derived from the Greek words agape, *meaning "love," and* anthos, *meaning "flower."*

Also called: lily-of-the-Nile **Features:** clump-forming habit; attractive foliage; mid- to late summer flowers **Flower color:** purple, blue, white **Height:** 12–36" **Spread:** 12–18" **Hardiness:** zones 7–10

Alstroemeria

Alstroemeria

Alstroemeria produces beautiful lily-like flowers over a long period. To encourage repeat blooms, pull the whole flowering shoot from the base rather than cutting the stem.

Growing

Alstroemeria grows well in **full sun** or **partial shade** in **well-drained** soil. Water regularly during the bloom season in early to midsummer. Alstroemeria goes dormant after bloom.

Tips

Alstroemeria is an exuberant companion in mixed borders. Flowers are bright, often with striped or blotched markings, and make long-lasting cut flowers.

Recommended

A. aurea grows 3–4' tall, sending up leafy shoots in spring followed by midsummer flowers in red, orange and pink with beautifully marked blossoms. Popular hybrids include **'Meyer'** and **'Inca.'**

Alstroemeria will last up to two weeks in a vase.

Also called: Peruvian lily **Features:** midsummer flowers; goes dormant after bloom **Flower color:** yellow, orange, red, salmon, pink; flecked markings **Height:** 2–6' **Spread:** 2–4' **Hardiness:** zones 6–10

Artemisia

Artemisia

Most artemisias are valued for their foliage, not their flowers. Silver is the ultimate blending color in the garden because it enhances every hue combined with it.

Growing

Artemisias grow best in **full sun**, in **well-drained** soil of **low to average fertility**. Rich soil causes lanky, invasive growth. Atemisias are very drought tolerant.

Artemisias respond well to pruning in late spring. When they look straggly, cut them back hard to encourage new growth and maintain a neater form. Divide these plants every year or two.

Tips

Use artemisias in rock gardens and borders. Their foliage makes a good backdrop for brightly colored flowers. Smaller forms may be used to create knot gardens.

Recommended

A variety of artemisias are available; check your local garden center.

***A. ludoviciana* cultivars** (white sage, silver sage) are vigorous, upright, clump-forming plants.

A. schmidtiana (silvermound artemisia) is a low, dense, mound-forming plant with feathery foliage. **'Nana'** (dwarf silvermound) is very compact.

A. stelleriana (beach wormwood) is a small plant that tolerates oceanside salt spray.

Also called: wormwood, sage **Features:** silvery gray, feathery or deeply lobed foliage **Flower color:** grown as a foliage plant **Height:** 6"–6' **Spread:** 12–36" **Hardiness:** zones 3–8

A. ludoviciana (above & below)

As far back as Roman times, artemisia has had a colorful history as an aphrodisiac, a medicinal plant and a key ingredient in absinthe.

Aster

Aster

A. novi-belgii (above & below)

Purple and pink asters make a nice contrast to the yellow-flowered perennials common in the late summer garden. You will have birds, butterflies and bees arriving for a late summer or fall garden party.

Growing

Asters prefer **full sun** but tolerate partial shade. The soil should be **fertile, moist** and **well drained**. In colder areas, mulch plants in winter to protect from temperature fluctuations.

Divide every two to three years to maintain vigor and control spread. Plants will decline rapidly if not divided frequently.

Tips

Plant asters in the middle of borders and in cottage gardens, or naturalize them in wild gardens.

In early spring and again in late spring, use hedge shears to cut back asters to create bushy, compact plants that don't need staking and have reduced disease problems.

Recommended

Many species and cultivars are available. The following are the two most popular species. Check with your local garden center to see what is available.

A. novae-angliae (Michaelmas daisy, New England aster) is an upright, spreading, clump-forming perennial that bears yellow-centered, purple flowers. The closely related Mexican daisy has white or pink flowers and makes an attractive, trailing ground cover.

A. novi-belgii (Michaelmas daisy, New York aster) is a dense, upright, clump-forming perennial with purple flowers.

Features: late summer to mid-fall flowers **Flower color:** red, white, blue, purple, pink; often with yellow centers **Height:** 10"–5' **Spread:** 18–36" **Hardiness:** zones 3–8

Astilbe

Astilbe

A. × *arendsii* (above & below)

Astilbes are beacons in the shade. Their high-impact flowers will brighten any gloomy section of your garden.

Growing

Astilbes grow best in **light shade** or **partial shade** in **fertile, humus-rich, acidic, moist, well-drained** soil. Heavy shade reduces flowering. Astilbes like moist soil in summer, but they should not sit in standing water during winter while they are dormant.

Astilbes should be divided every three years or so to maintain plant vigor. Root masses may lift out of the soil as they mature. Add a layer of topsoil and mulch if this occurs, or lift the entire plant and replant it deeper.

Tips

Astilbes can be grown near the edges of bog gardens and ponds, in woodland gardens and shaded borders.

Recommended

A.* × *arendsii (astilbe, false spirea, Arend's astilbe) is a group of hybrids with many available cultivars.

A. chinensis (Chinese astilbe) is a dense, vigorous perennial that tolerates dry soil better than other astilbe species. Many cultivars are available.

A. japonica (Japanese astilbe) is a compact, clump-forming species, rarely grown in favor of its many cultivars.

In late summer, transplant seedlings found near the parent plant to create plumes of color all through the garden.

Features: attractive foliage; summer flowers; interesting seedheads **Flower color:** white, pink, purple, peach, red **Height:** 10"–4' **Spread:** 8–36" **Hardiness:** zones 3–8

Black-Eyed Susan

Rudbeckia

R. fulgida with purple coneflower (above), *R. nitida* 'Herbstonne' (below)

Black-eyed Susan is a tough, low-maintenance, long-lived perennial. Plant it wherever you want a casual look.

Growing

Black-eyed Susans grow well in **full sun** or **partial shade**. The soil should be of **average fertility** and **well drained**. Some *Rudbeckia* species are touted as "claybusters" for their tolerance of fairly heavy clay soils. Established plants are drought tolerant but appreciate regular water.

Divide black-eyed Susans in spring or fall, every three to five years. Pinching the plants in June will result in shorter, bushier stands.

Tips

Include these native plants in wildflower and natural gardens, beds and borders. Black-eyed Susans look great in drifts.

Recommended

R. fulgida is an upright, spreading plant bearing orange-yellow flowers with brown centers. **Var. *sullivantii* 'Goldsturm'** bears large, golden yellow flowers.

R. laciniata (cutleaf coneflower) forms a large, open clump. The yellow flowers have green centers. **'Goldquelle'** has bright yellow, double flowers.

R. nitida is an upright, spreading plant with green-centered, yellow flowers. **'Herbstonne'** ('Autumn Sun') has golden yellow flowers.

The flowers last well when cut for arrangements.

Features: bright flowers; attractive foliage; easy to grow **Flower color:** yellow, orange, red; centers typically brown or green **Height:** 24"–6' **Spread:** 18–36" **Hardiness:** zones 3–8

Catmint

Nepeta

H. × *faassenii* (above & below)

The real workhorses of the garden bed, catmints offer season-long blooms on sturdy, trouble-free plants.

Growing

These plants prefer **full sun** in coastal areas and **partial shade** inland. Grow them in **well-drained** soil of **average fertility**; the growth tends to flop in rich soil.

Plant in spring and divide in spring or fall when they look overgrown and dense. In June, pinch the tips to delay flowering and to make the plants more compact.

Tips

Catmints form upright, spreading clumps. Plant them in herb gardens, perennial beds, rock gardens and cottage gardens with roses. Or use them to edge borders and pathways.

Like all members of the mint family, catmint has square stems.

Recommended

N. 'Blue Beauty' (Souvenir d'André Chaudron) has gray-green foliage and large, dark, purple-blue flowers.

N. ×*faassenii* bears blue or purple flowers. Cultivars with gray-green foliage and pink, white, light purple or lavender blue flowers are available, as well as low-growing cultivars.

N. 'Six Hills Giant' bears deep lavender blue flowers.

Take care if you decide to grow N. cataria *(catnip) because cats are extremely attracted to this plant. Cats do like the other species, but not as much.*

Features: aromatic foliage; attractive flowers; easy to grow **Flower color:** blue, purple, white, pink **Height:** 18–36" **Spread:** 12–24" **Hardiness:** zones 3–8

Columbine

Aquilegia

A. vulgaris (above), *A.* × *hybrida* (below)

Delicate but long-lasting columbine flowers herald the passing of spring and the arrival of warm summer weather.

Growing

Columbines grow well in **full sun** or **partial shade**. They prefer **fertile, moist, well-drained** soil, but they adapt to most soil conditions.

Division is not required but can be done to propagate desirable plants. The divided plants may take a while to recover because columbines dislike having their roots disturbed.

Tips

Use columbines in rock gardens, formal or casual borders and naturalized or woodland gardens.

Recommended

A. alpina has blue flowers.

A.* × *hybrida (*A.* × *cultorum*; hybrid columbine) has exceptional flowers. Hybrids in a wide range of colors have been developed.

A. vulgaris (common columbine, European columbine) has been used to develop many hybrids and cultivars with flowers in various colors.

Columbines self-seed but are not invasive. Each year, a few new seedlings may turn up near the parent plant and can be transplanted.

Features: spring and summer flowers; attractive foliage **Flower color:** red, yellow, pink, purple, blue, white; color of spurs often differs from that of petals **Height:** 18–36" **Spread:** 12–24" **Hardiness:** zones 3–8

Coral Bells

Heuchera

These delicate woodland plants will enhance your garden with their bright colors, attractive foliage and airy sprays of flowers.

Growing

Grow coral bells in **partial shade** or **full sun** in cooler, moderate climates. Soil should be **average to fertile, neutral to slightly alkaline, evenly moist** and **well drained**. Deadhead to prolong the blooming period.

Coral bells may push themselves up out of the soil. Mulch plants in fall if they begin heaving from the ground.

Every two or three years in spring or fall, dig up plants to remove the oldest, woodiest roots and stems. Divide the plants at this time if desired, then replant the crowns just above soil level.

Features: colorful foliage; easy to grow **Flower color:** red, pink, white **Height:** 12" **Spread:** 12" **Hardiness:** zones 3–8

Tips

Use coral bells as edging plants, in clusters in woodland gardens or as groundcovers in low-traffic areas. Combine different foliage types for an interesting display.

Recommended

Many coral bells species, cultivars and hybrids exist, providing a range of sizes, flower colors and foliage colors and shapes. Check with your local garden center or nursery.

Cut flowers of Heuchera *(pronounced hew-ker-uh) can be used in arrangements.*

Daylily

Hemerocallis

The daylily's adaptability and durability, combined with its variety in color, blooming period, size and texture, explain its popularity.

Growing

Daylilies grow in any light from **full sun to partial shade**. The deeper the shade, the fewer flowers will be produced. The soil should be **fertile, moist** and **well drained**.

These plants adapt to most conditions and are hard to kill once established. Divide every two to three years to keep plants vigorous and to propagate them. They can be left indefinitely without dividing. Deadhead to prolong blooming.

Tips

Plant daylilies alone, or group them in borders, on banks and in ditches to control erosion. They can be naturalized in woodland or meadow gardens. Small varieties look nice in planters.

Be careful when deadheading purple-flowered daylilies because the sap can stain fingers and clothes.

Easygoing, adaptive and versatile, daylilies are so tough they can even be dug up and moved while in full bloom.

Recommended

Daylilies come in an almost infinite number of forms, sizes and colors, in a range of species, cultivars and hybrids. See your local garden center or daylily grower to find out what's available and what suits your garden.

Features: spring and summer flowers; grass-like foliage; easy to grow **Flower color:** every color except blue and pure white **Height:** 12"–4' **Spread:** 12"–4' **Hardiness:** zones 2–8

Euphorbia

Euphorbia

E. griffithii 'Fireglow' (above), *E. polychroma* (below)

These mounding plants are admired for the brightly colored bracts that surround their tiny flowers. A second show of color appears in fall when the leaves turn purple, red or orange.

Growing

Euphorbia grows well in **full sun** or **light shade**, in **moist, well-drained, humus-rich** soil of **average fertility**. This plant is drought tolerant and can be invasive in fertile soil. It does not tolerate wet conditions.

Division is rarely required. Euphorbia dislikes being disturbed once established. Propagate euphorbia with stem cuttings. Dip the cut ends in hot water to stop the sticky white sap from running. Plant them in spring or fall.

Tips

Use euphorbia in a mixed or herbaceous border, rock garden or lightly shaded woodland garden.

Also called: cushion spurge **Features:** colorful bracts; fall foliage; low maintenance **Flower color:** yellow **Height:** 12–24" **Spread:** 18–24" **Hardiness:** zones 4–8

Recommended

E. characias produces striking chartreuse flowers on tall plants.

***E. griffithii* 'Fireglow'** has light green leaves, orange stems and bright orange bracts.

E. polychroma (*E. epithimoides*) has inconspicuous flowers surrounded by long-lasting, yellow bracts. It has several cultivars.

You may wish to wear gloves when handling this plant because the sap contains latex, which can irritate the skin.

Foamflower

Tiarella

T. cordifolia (above & below)

Foamflowers form handsome groundcovers in shaded areas, with their attractive leaves and delicate, starry, white flowers.

Growing

Foamflowers prefer **partial, light or full shade** without afternoon sun. The soil should be **humus rich, moist** and **slightly acidic**. These plants adapt to most soils.

Divide in spring. Deadhead to encourage reblooming. If the foliage fades or rusts in summer, cut it partway to the ground. New growth will emerge.

Tips

Foamflowers are excellent groundcovers for shaded and woodland gardens. They can be included in shaded borders and left to naturalize in wild gardens.

Recommended

T. cordifolia is a low-growing, spreading plant that bears spikes of foamy looking, white flowers.

***T.* 'Maple Leaf'** is a clump-forming hybrid with bronze-green, maple-like leaves and pink-flushed flowers.

New varieties of foamflowers are flooding the market with spectacular leaf color. Some have bands, splotches and rings.

Don't worry about foamflower taking over the garden. It spreads rather politely by underground stolons and is easily pulled up if it wanders too enthusiastically.

Features: spring and sometimes early summer flowers; decorative foliage **Flower color:** white, pink **Height:** 4–24" **Spread:** 12–24" **Hardiness:** zones 3–8

Fortnight Lily

Dietes

This plant is a reliable bloomer—every fortnight, or two weeks—with iris-like flowers and narrow, evergreen leaves. In mild climates, fortnight lily blooms year round. Flowers last for only a day.

D. hybrid (above & below)

Growing

Fortnight lily does well in **full sun** or **partial shade** in **average, well-drained** soil. It will survive and bloom, however, even with a certain amount of neglect.

Tips

Place fortnight lilies in areas where you don't want a lot of fuss and bother. These attractive plants last for years and mix well with other plants.

Recommended

D. bicolor is a South African species that grows 24–36" tall and has yellow flowers with brown markings.

***D.* hybrids** with various flower colors are also available.

To encourage more blooms, remove the flower stalk after the blossom fades.

Also called: African iris **Features:** evergreen foliage; iris-like flowers **Flower color:** white, cream, yellow **Height:** 24–36" **Spread:** 24–36" **Hardiness:** zones 8–10

Golden Marguerite

Anthemis

Grow golden marguerite to give your garden a casual cottage appearance.

Growing

Golden marguerite prefers **full sun** and **average to poor, well-drained** soil. This plant is drought tolerant.

Golden marguerite flowers in waves. Deadheading will encourage flowering all summer and greatly reduce self-seeding. Cut back thin-looking plants to promote new growth and flowers. To avoid staking, cut plants back in May or group several plants to support each other. To support the stems as they grow, insert twiggy branches into the soil around the plants when they are young.

The clumps tend to die out in the middle and should be divided every two or three years in spring or fall. Plant them in spring.

Tips

Marguerites form attractive clumps that blend wonderfully into cottage-style gardens. Their drought tolerance makes them ideal for use in rock gardens and on exposed slopes.

Golden marguerites look great as cut flowers placed in anything from vases to tin cans and old teapots.

Recommended

A. tinctoria forms a mounded clump of foliage that becomes completely covered in daisy-like flowers in summer. Its cultivars bloom in shades of orange and yellow.

Also called: marguerite daisy **Features:** colorful flowers **Flower color:** yellow, orange, cream **Height:** 24–36" **Spread:** 24–36" **Hardiness:** zones 3–7

Hardy Geranium

Geranium

G. sanguineum (above & below)

Thanks to the beauty and diversity of this hardy plant, there is a type of geranium that suits every garden.

Growing

Hardy geraniums grow well in **full sun, partial shade** or **light shade**. These plants dislike hot weather and prefer **well-drained** soil of **average fertility**. *G. renardii* prefers a poor, well-drained soil.

Shear back spent flowers for a second set of blooms. Rejuvenate ratty foliage by pruning in late summer. Divide in spring.

Tips

These long-flowering plants work well in a border; they fill in the spaces between shrubs and other large plants and keep weeds down. Include them in rock gardens and woodland gardens, or mass plant them as groundcovers.

Also called: cranesbill geranium **Features:** summer flowers; attractive, sometimes fragrant foliage **Flower color:** white, red, pink, purple, blue **Height:** 4–36" **Spread:** 12–36" **Hardiness:** zones 3–8

Recommended

***G.* 'Brookside'** is a clump-forming, drought-tolerant geranium with finely cut leaves and deep blue to violet blue flowers.

G. macrorrhizum (bigroot geranium, scented cranesbill) forms a spreading mound of fragrant foliage with flowers in various shades of pink.

G. renardii (Renard's geranium) forms a clump of velvety, deeply veined, crinkled foliage. A few purple-veined, white flowers appear over summer.

G. sanguineum (bloodred cranesbill, bloody cranesbill) forms a dense, mounding clump and bears bright magenta flowers.

Hosta

Hosta

Some gardeners think the flowers clash with the foliage, so they remove the newly emerged flower stems. Doing so won't harm the plant.

Breeders are always looking for new variations in hosta foliage. Swirls, stripes, puckers and ribs enhance the leaves' various sizes, shapes and colors.

Growing

Hostas prefer **light shade** or **partial shade** but will grow in full shade. Morning sun is preferable to afternoon sun. The soil should ideally be **fertile, moist** and **well drained**, but most soils are tolerated. Hostas are fairly drought tolerant, especially if mulched to help retain moisture. Hostas do not thrive in southern California.

Division is not required but can be done every few years in spring or summer to propagate new plants.

Tips

Hostas make wonderful woodland plants and look very attractive when combined with ferns and other fine-textured plants. Hostas work well in mixed borders, particularly when used to hide leggy lower stems and branches of some shrubs.

Hostas' dense growth and thick, shade-providing leaves help suppress weeds; however, the plants attract slugs and snails, so be sure to use a bait that is not toxic to pets.

Recommended

There are hundreds of hosta species, cultivars and hybrids. Visit your local garden center or get a mail-order catalog to find out what's available.

Also called: plantain lily **Features:** decorative foliage; summer and fall flowers **Flower color:** white, purple; grown mainly as a foliage plant **Height:** 4–36" **Spread:** 6"–6' **Hardiness:** zones 3–8

Iris

Iris

Irises are old-fashioned flowers that bring back childhood memories of Grandma's spring garden.

Growing

Irises prefer **full sun** but tolerate very light or dappled shade. The soil should be of **average fertility** and **well drained**. Japanese iris and Siberian iris prefer moist, well-drained soil.

Divide irises in late summer or early fall. Deadhead to keep them tidy. Cut back Siberian iris' foliage in spring.

Tips

All irises are popular border plants. Japanese and Siberian iris grow well alongside streams or ponds. Dwarf cultivars look attractive in rock gardens.

Irises can cause severe internal irritation if ingested. Always wash your hands after handling them. Avoid planting irises where children play.

I. siberica (above), bearded iris (below)

Cut bearded iris foliage to within a few inches of the ground in midsummer to discourage leaf spot and other fungal diseases.

Recommended

Many species and hybrids are available. Among the most popular is **bearded iris**, often a hybrid of ***I. germanica***. It has the widest range of flower colors but is susceptible to iris borer. Several irises are not susceptible, including ***I. ensata*** (Japanese iris) and ***I. siberica*** (Siberian iris). **Pacific Coast hybrids** come in many colors and sizes.

Features: spring, summer and sometimes fall flowers; attractive foliage **Flower color:** many shades of pink, red, purple, blue, white, brown, yellow **Height:** 4"–4' **Spread:** 2"–4' **Hardiness:** zones 3–8

Lamium

Lamium

'Limelight' (above), 'Beacon Silver' (below)

With its striking, variegated leaves, lamium brightens up dark spaces in the garden. It looks especially lovely at dusk and in the moonlight.

Growing

Lamium prefers **partial shade** or **light shade**. It tolerates full shade but may grow leggy. The soil should be of **average fertility, humus rich, moist** and **well drained**. The more fertile the soil, the more vigorously the plant will grow. Plant in spring or fall.

Lamium is drought tolerant when grown in shade, but it can develop bare patches if the soil is allowed to dry out for extended periods. Divide and replant it in fall if bare spots become unsightly.

Tips

Lamium makes a useful groundcover in woodland or shade gardens. Or try planting it under shrubs in a border, where it will help keep weeds down.

Recommended

L. maculatum (spotted dead nettle) is a low-growing, spreading plant with white, pink or mauve flowers. Many cultivars are available.

Lamium will remain more compact if sheared back after flowering. If the plant becomes invasive, pull some of it up. Make sure to remove the fleshy roots.

Also called: dead nettle, spotted dead nettle **Features:** foliage; flowers **Flower color:** white, pink, red-purple **Height:** 8" **Spread:** 36" **Hardiness:** zones 3–8

Lantana

Lantana

If you need a tough plant that's almost constantly in flower, consider lantana. This evergreen perennial has small flowers in shades ranging from sedate lavender to a wild combo of yellow and hot pink.

L. 'Red Spread' (above), *L. montevidensis* (below)

Growing

Lantana prefers **full sun** in **average, well-drained** soil. Provide with moderate water until established, and then water infrequently but deeply. While it will tolerate some chill, hard frost may kill it.

Tips

Lantana can be used in a variety of ways—as a shrub, groundcover, hedge, or hanging plant. Spreading lantana is an easy, attractive way to cover a bank or other hard-to-tend area because it requires little care.

Recommended

***L.* hybrids** are available in a variety of heights and colors. All are sturdy and relatively low maintenance. The **Patriot Series** is a low (12–15" tall) but wide (4–5') spreader with multi-colored flowers in shades of yellow, pink, orange and red. Cheerful **'Confetti'** is a mix of yellow, pink and purple blossoms that can grow 3' tall and 8' wide.

L. montevidensis is a trailing groundcover that grows about 22" tall and spreads up to 36", with purple or purple-and-white flowers. Dark green leaves may develop a red or purple cast during cold weather.

Lantana is toxic if ingested.

Features: small, colorful flowers; fast growing; evergreen where hardy **Flower color:** yellow, pink, red, orange, purple, white **Height:** 12"–5' **Spread:** 24"–8' **Hardiness:** zones 4–11

Lewisia

Lewisia

Native to the west coast, lewisia was discovered by and named for famous explorer Meriwether Lewis. It is the perfect succulent for California gardens.

Growing

Plant succulents in **full sun** or **partial shade** in very **well-drained** soil. Let soil dry out between waterings. To start a new plant, break off a stem and stick it in well-drained soil.

Some succulents are frost tender; in areas where freezing temperatures are common, overwinter lewisia inside. Elsewhere, protect it from excessive winter moisture.

Tips

Succulent choice and use are largely dependent on climate. In California, succulents are widely used as ground covers and accent plants in places that are difficult to irrigate. Lewisia is particularly attractive in a rock garden.

Succulents are available in a wide range of sizes, colors and shapes and deliver a lot of payback for little care, requiring only occasional water, sun and well-drained soil.

Recommended

L. cotyledon is a flowering evergreen succulent native to northern California. Pink, purple, yellow or white, 2" flowers appear in spring and summer. Prolific bloomer **Rainbow Mix** has white, pink, peach and purple flowers.

Also called: bitterroot, cliff maids **Features:** fleshy, evergreen foliage; spring to midsummer flowers **Flower color:** pink, white, yellow, purple, peach; also bicolored **Height:** 6–18" **Spread:** 6–12" **Hardiness:** zones 3–8

Penstemon

Penstemon

'Husker Red' (above), 'Apple Blossom' (below)

Penstemon's colorful stalks will welcome hummingbirds and butterflies on a summer day.

Growing

Penstemons prefer **full sun** but tolerate some shade. The soil should be of **average to rich fertility, sandy** and **well drained**. Penstemons are drought tolerant and will rot in wet soil. Plant in spring or fall; divide every two or three years in spring.

Insert twiggy branches in the soil around the plants in spring before they grow too tall. Pinch plants when they reach 12" tall to encourage bushy growth.

Tips

The attractive flowers make a lovely addition to a mixed border, cottage garden or rock garden.

Recommended

Penstemon has many species, cultivars and hybrids, which provide a range of flower colors, shapes and sizes. Check at your local garden center for availability.

P. digitalis **'Husker Red'** is a recent Perennial Plant Association Perennial Plant of the Year. The bronze-red foliage contrasts well with its white flowers.

P. eatonii **'Scarlet Firecracker'** is a good choice in hot regions.

P. **hybrids 'Apple Blossom,' 'Midnight'** and **'Sour Grapes'** are reliable bloomers in summer on bushy, well-formed plants.

Give penstemons a bit of compost in spring and fall.

Also called: beard tongue **Features:** interesting flowers **Flower color:** white, yellow, light pink, rose pink, purple **Height:** 8–24" **Spread:** 10–12" **Hardiness:** zones 4–9

Peony

Paeonia

From the simple single flowers to the extravagant doubles, it's easy to become mesmerized by these voluptuous plants. The foliage remains stellar throughout the growing season.

Growing

Peonies prefer **full sun** but tolerate some shade. They do best in areas with some winter chill. Peonies like **fertile, humus-rich, moist, well-drained** soil with lots of compost. Prepare the soil before planting. Mulch peonies lightly with compost in spring. Too much fertilizer, particularly nitrogen, causes floppy growth and retards blooming.

Peony tubers planted too shallow or too deep will not flower. The buds or eyes on the tuber should be 1½–2" below the soil surface. Place wire tomato or peony cages around the plants in early spring to support the heavy flowers. The growing foliage will hide the cage. Deadhead to keep plants looking tidy. Peonies don't appreciate being divided.

Tips

Peonies look great in a border combined with other early bloomers. Avoid planting peonies under trees, where they have to compete for moisture and nutrients.

Recommended

Hundreds of peony varieties exist. Cultivars come in a wide range of colors, may have single or double flowers and may or may not be fragrant. Visit your local garden center to see what is available.

Features: spring and early summer flowers; attractive foliage **Flower color:** white, cream, yellow, pink, red, purple **Height:** 24–36" **Spread:** 24–36" **Hardiness:** zones 2–8

Phlox

Phlox

Phlox comes in many shapes and sizes, from low creepers to bushy border plants. Its flowering periods can fall anywhere between early spring and mid-fall.

Growing

P. maculata and *P. paniculata* prefer **full sun**; *P. subulata* prefers **full sun to partial shade**; *P. stolonifera* prefers **light to partial shade** but tolerates heavy shade. All phloxes like **fertile, humus-rich, moist, well-drained** soil. Divide in fall or spring.

Tips

Low-growing species are useful in rock gardens or at the front of borders. Taller phloxes may be used in the middle of borders and are particularly effective planted in groups.

P. paniculata (above & below)

Recommended

P. maculata (early phlox, garden phlox, wild sweet William) forms an upright clump of hairy stems and narrow leaves that are sometimes spotted with red. Pink, purple or white flowers are borne in conical clusters.

P. paniculata (garden phlox, summer phlox) is an upright plant. Its many cultivars vary in size and flower color.

P. stolonifera (creeping phlox) is a low, spreading plant that bears flowers in several shades of purple.

P. subulata (moss phlox, moss pink) is very low growing and bears flowers in various colors. The foliage is evergreen.

Features: spring, summer or fall flowers **Flower color:** white, blue, purple, orange, pink, red **Height:** 2"–4' **Spread:** 12–36" **Hardiness:** zones 3–8

Pink

Dianthus

D. deltoides (above), *D. plumarius* (below)

From tiny and delicate to large and robust, this genus contains a wide variety of plants, many with spicy scented flowers.

Growing

Pinks prefer **full sun** but tolerate some light shade. A **well-drained, neutral to alkaline** soil is required. Ensure pinks have excellent drainage—they hate to stand in water.

To prolong blooming, deadhead as the flowers fade, but leave a few flowers in place to go to seed.

Tips

Use pinks in rock gardens and rock walls, for edging borders and walkways, in cutting gardens and even as a groundcover.

Recommended

D. × allwoodii (allwood pink) forms a compact mound and bears flowers in a wide range of colors. Many cultivars are available.

D. deltoides (maiden pink) forms a mat of foliage and flowers in shades of red.

D. gratianopolitanus (cheddar pink) is long lived and forms a very dense mat of evergreen, silvery gray foliage with sweet-scented flowers mostly in shades of pink.

D. plumarius (cottage pink) is noted for its role in the development of garden pink. The flowers can be single, semi-double or fully double and come in many colors.

Pinks self-seed quite easily. Seedlings may differ from the parent plants, often with new and interesting results.

Features: sometimes-fragrant, spring or summer flowers; attractive foliage **Flower color:** pink, red, white, purple **Height:** 2–18" **Spread:** 6–24" **Hardiness:** zones 3–9

Primrose

Primula

Planted among dwarf daffodils, lungworts and pulmonarias, primroses add to a tapestry of woodland flowers. They are the jewels of the spring display.

Growing

Grow primrose in **partial shade**, in **moderately fertile, humus-rich, moist, well-drained, neutral to slightly acidic** soil. If the temperature is too hot or too cold, primroses will stop blooming. Plant them in a variety of sites to increase your chances of success.

Pull off yellowing or dried leaves in fall to encourage fresh, new growth in spring. Overgrown clumps should be divided after flowering or in early fall. Plant in spring.

Tips

Primroses work well in many areas of the garden. Some prefer woodland areas while others thrive in moisture. Species with flowers on tall stems look excellent in masses, while species with solitary flowers peeking out among the foliage add an interesting dimension to the garden.

Recommended

The most popular primroses are **Polyantha Hybrids**, which are available in a wide range of solid colors or bicolors. Many species and cultivars are available, with colorful flowers and a variety of plant forms.

Primroses thrive with some winter chill and make cheerful additions to northern California gardens.

Features: colorful flowers; variety of forms **Flower color:** red, orange, pink, purple, blue, white, yellow **Height:** 6–24" **Spread:** 6–18" **Hardiness:** zones 3–8

Purple Coneflower

Echinacea

Purple coneflower is a visual delight, with its mauve petals offset by a spiky, orange center.

Growing

Purple coneflower grows well in **full sun** or very **light shade**. It tolerates any **well-drained** soil, but prefers an **average to rich** soil. Thick taproots make this plant drought resistant, but it prefers to have regular water.

Deadhead early in the season to prolong flowering. Later, you may wish to leave the flowerheads in place to self-seed and provide winter interest. Pinch plants back or thin out the stems in early summer to encourage bushy growth that is less prone to mildew. Divide every four years or so in spring or fall.

Tips

Use purple coneflower in meadow gardens and informal borders, in groups or as a single specimen. The dry flowerheads make an interesting feature in fall and winter gardens.

Recommended

E. purpurea is an upright plant covered in prickly hairs. It bears purple flowers with rusty orange centers. Cultivars are available.

Purple coneflower attracts wildlife to the garden; it provides pollen, nectar and seeds for various hungry visitors.

Features: midsummer to fall flowers; persistent seedheads **Flower color:** purple, pink, white; orange centers **Height:** 24"–5' **Spread:** 12–24" **Hardiness:** zones 3–8

Sea Pink

Armeria

Sea pink is the perfect plant to grow in pots at an oceanside cabin, where it can add tufts of texture to a sunny rock garden or alongside a flagstone path. This tough perennial can survive neglect.

Growing

Sea pink requires **full sun**. Soil should be **poor to moderate** and **well drained**. Sea pink is very drought tolerant.

If it seems to be dying out in the middle of the clump, try cutting it back hard. New shoots should fill in quickly. Plant sea pink in spring and divide it in spring or fall.

Tips

Sea pink is great for seaside gardens because it tolerates salt spray. Use this little gem in a rock garden or at the front of a border. The rounded blossoms blend well with other drought-tolerant plants with gray foliage.

A. maritima (above & below)

Recommended

***A.* 'Bee's Ruby'** is a larger cultivar with bright pink flowers.

A. maritima is the most common and most variable sea pink. The flowering stems rise above the tufts of foliage.

Attract bees and butterflies to a seaside garden with clumps of dependable sea pinks.

Also called: common thrift **Features:** flowers; foliage; salt tolerance **Flower color:** shades of pink, red, white **Height:** 6–18" **Spread:** 8–12" **Hardiness:** zones 3–8

Wild Ginger

Asarum

A. canadense (above), *A. europaeum* (below)

Wild ginger flowers have a unique shape, an unusual brown-red color and an unpleasant, slightly fetid odor that attracts their beetle pollinators.

Wild ginger is a beautiful groundcover for woodland sites. Glossy, heart-shaped leaves form a low-growing mat that grows quickly but is not invasive.

Growing

Wild gingers need **partial to full shade**. The soil should be **moist** and **humus rich**. All *Asarum* species prefer **acidic** soils, but *A. canadense* will tolerate alkaline conditions. Wild gingers tolerate dry conditions for a while in good shade, but prolonged drought will eventually cause wilt and dieback.

Tips

Use wild ginger in a shady rock garden, border or woodland garden. Wild ginger is relatively easy to remove from places where it isn't welcome.

Recommended

A. canadense (Canada wild ginger) has slightly hairy, heart-shaped leaves. The roots of this wild ginger can be used in place of true ginger (*Zingiber officinale*) in recipes.

A. caudatum (British Columbia wild ginger) prefers cooler summer growing conditions.

A. europaeum (European wild ginger) forms an expanding clump of glossy leaves, often distinctively silver-veined. This species is not as heat tolerant as *A. canadense*.

Features: attractive foliage; inconspicuous flowers; easy to grow **Flower color:** burgundy, green; grown as a foliage plant **Height:** 3–6" **Spread:** 12" or more **Hardiness:** zones 4–8

Arborvitae

Thuja

Arborvitae makes a gorgeous backdrop for perennial and shrub borders. Rot-resistant, durable and long-lived, arborvitae has earned the admiration of gardeners everywhere.

P. *occidentalis* 'Yellow Ribbon' (above), P. *occidentalis* (below)

Growing

Arborvitae grows well in **full sun, partial shade** or **light shade** in a **sheltered** location. The soil should be of **average fertility, moist** and **well drained**. These plants enjoy humidity and grow well near marshy areas. Provide some shelter from strong or frequent winds.

Tips

Larger varieties of arborvitae make excellent specimen trees. Smaller cultivars can be used in foundation plantings, in shrub and mixed borders, as formal or informal hedges and in rock gardens. Varieties with yellow foliage add color to the winter landscape.

Recommended

T. occidentalis (American arborvitae, eastern arborvitae) is a dense, broad, pyramidal tree. (Zones 2–7; cultivars are not always this cold hardy)

T. orientalis (*Platycladus orientalis*, Oriental arborvitae) is a pyramidal to columnar, large shrub or small tree. (Zones 5–8)

T. plicata (western red cedar, western arborvitae) is a very large, often multi-stemmed, narrow, pyramidal tree. (Zones 5–7)

The pungent oils in this tree's foliage may irritate sensitive skin.

Deer enjoy eating the foliage of eastern arborvitae. Western arborvitae is relatively resistant to deer browsing.

Also called: cedar **Features:** foliage; bark; form **Habit:** small to large, evergreen tree **Height:** 3–75' **Spread:** 3–25' **Hardiness:** zones 2–8

Arbutus

Arbutus

A. menziesii (above & below)

Arbutus trees grow wild along the Pacific coast, often on rocky cliffs overlooking the water. The peeling bark, interesting twisted and irregular forms, clusters of white flowers in early summer and bright red fruit that attracts plenty of birds provide more than enough reason to grow this Pacific beauty.

Growing

Arbutus prefers a **sheltered** spot in **full sun.** The soil should be **fertile, humus rich** and **well drained**. Avoid overwatering these trees, which are drought and salt tolerant. Pruning is not usually required.

Arbutus does not like having its roots disturbed. Plant young stock and make sure the location is a permanent one.

Tips

Use arbutus in a woodland garden or as a specimen tree. Include the smaller cultivars in shrub or mixed borders.

Recommended

***A.* 'Marina'** has large, green leaves, rosy pink flowers and red and yellow fruit.

A. menziesii (arbutus, Pacific madrone) is a large, spreading or shrubby tree with distinctive reddish bark that continuously peels off to reveal smooth, greenish young bark underneath.

A. unedo (Mediterranean strawberry tree) is a spreading, shrubby tree with shredding, exfoliating red-brown bark.

Birds love arbutus fruits, but people can suffer stomachaches if they eat too many.

Also called: strawberry tree, madrone **Features:** flowers; fruit; bark; form **Habit:** spreading or shrubby, broad-leaved, evergreen tree **Height:** 5–70' **Spread:** 5–70' **Hardiness:** zones 7–8

Barberry

Berberis

B. darwinii (above), *B. thunbergii* (below)

Barberries are dependable, easy-growing shrubs with many variations in plant size, foliage color and fruit.

Growing

Barberries develop the best fall color and most fruit when grown in **full sun**, but they tolerate partial shade. Any **well-drained** soil is suitable. Barberries tolerate drought and urban conditions but suffer in poorly drained, wet soil.

Tips

Large barberries make great hedges. They can also be included in shrub and mixed borders. Small cultivars can be grown in rock gardens, in raised beds and along rock walls.

Recommended

B. darwinii (Darwin's barberry) bears small, yellow flowers in spring and often again in fall, and small, dark blue berries. This evergreen species is not as spiny as others.

B.* × *mentorensis (Mentor barberry) is a large, generally deciduous shrub with even, dense growth, impassable spines, yellow, spring flowers and attractive fall color.

B. thunbergii (Japanese barberry) is a broad, rounded, dense shrub with bright green foliage, yellow, spring flowers, glossy, red fruit and orange, red or purple fall color. Many cultivars have varied foliage color, including shades of purple and yellow. Variegated varieties also exist.

With its graceful, arching branches and often colorful foliage, barberry makes an attractive addition to the garden year-round, while its thorns provide a measure of privacy.

Features: foliage; flowers; fruit; formidable spines **Habit:** prickly, deciduous shrub **Height:** 12"–6' **Spread:** 18"–6' **Hardiness:** zones 4–8

Birch

Betula

'Youngii' (above), 'Trost' (below)

Birch trees are a graceful addition to any garden. Even after the leaves have dropped, the drooping branches and white bark are attractive and look great year-round.

Growing

Birches prefer **full sun** or **partial shade** and **well-drained** soil. Be sure to give them regular water. To keep birches' shallow roots cool, make sure to mulch.

Tips

Multi-trunk varieties are attractive and create a noteworthy presence in the garden, particularly if you have room for only one tree.

Recommended

B. pendula (European white birch) is the most commonly planted birch. It is available in a variety of heights and leaf colors. Check with a reliable nursery to discover a variety that does well in your region.

Birches can occasionally attract pests such as aphids and borers.

Features: foliage, bark **Habit:** open, airy, deciduous tree **Height:** 30–70' **Spread:** 15–25' **Hardiness:** zones 2–8

Bluebeard

Caryopteris

Bluebeard is a cheerful, easy-to-grow shrub that will wake up a late-summer border with its blue flowers. The flowers and foliage contrast superbly with purple-leaved plants.

Growing

Bluebeard prefers **full sun** but tolerates light shade. It does best in soil of **average fertility** that is **light** and **well drained**.

Tips

Include bluebeard in your shrub or mixed border. This plant can be treated as a herbaceous perennial in areas where it is killed back each winter.

Recommended

C. × clandonensis forms a dense mound and bears clusters of blue or purple flowers in late summer and early fall. **'Blue Mist'** is a low-growing, mounding plant with fragrant, light blue flowers. **'Worcester Gold'** has bright yellow-green foliage that contrasts vividly with the violet-blue, late summer flowers.

Bluebeard is cultivated for its aromatic stems, foliage and flowers.

Also called: bluebird, blue spirea **Features:** flowers; foliage; scent **Habit:** rounded, spreading, deciduous shrub **Height:** 24–36" **Spread:** 2–6' **Hardiness:** zones 5–8

Boxwood

Buxus

B. sempervirens (above & below)

Boxwoods can be pruned to form neat hedges, geometric shapes or fanciful creatures. When allowed to grow naturally, boxwoods form attractive, rounded mounds.

Growing

Boxwoods prefer to grow in **partial shade**, but they tolerate full sun if kept well watered. The soil should be **fertile, moist** and **well drained**. Mulching will benefit these shrubs.

Boxwood foliage contains toxic compounds that, when ingested, can cause severe digestive upset and possibly death.

Tips

Boxwoods have many wonderful qualities, but a pleasant scent isn't one of them. They make excellent background plants in mixed borders.

Recommended

B. microphylla (littleleaf boxwood) is quite pest resistant and hardy in zones 6–8. The foliage tends to lose its green in winter. ***B. m.* var. *koreana*** is hardy and survives where others may freeze.

B. sempervirens (common boxwood) is a larger species with foliage that stays green in winter. Cultivars are available with interesting features such as compact or dwarf growth, variegated foliage and pendulous branches. It is not a good choice for hot summer regions.

Several cultivars developed from crossing ***B. m.* var. *koreana*** and ***B. sempervirens*** exhibit good hardiness and pest resistance and have attractive year-round foliage.

Also called: box **Features:** foliage; slow, even growth **Habit:** dense, rounded, evergreen shrub **Height:** 3–15' **Spread:** equal to height **Hardiness:** zones 4–8

Butterfly Bush

Buddleia (Buddleja)

Butterfly bushes are among the best shrubs for attracting butterflies and bees to a garden. Don't spray your bush for pests—you will harm its beautiful and beneficial insects.

Growing

Butterfly bushes prefer to grow in **full sun**. Plants grown in shade will produce few flowers. The soil should be **average to fertile** and **well drained**. These shrubs are drought tolerant once established.

To control this very fast-growing shrub, cut it back heavily in spring, leaving just one-foot stumps. It will bloom that same summer.

Tips

Its graceful, arching branches make butterfly bush an excellent specimen plant and a beautiful addition to shrub and mixed borders.

B. davidii (above & below)

Recommended

B. alternifolia (alternate-leaved butterfly bush) can be trained to form a small tree. In late spring or early summer, clusters of light purple flowers form on the ends of the branches.

B. davidii (orange-eye butterfly bush, summer lilac) bears flowers in bright and pastel shades of purple, white, pink or blue from midsummer to fall. Many cultivars are available. (Zones 5–8)

Butterfly bush can self-seed. You may find tiny bushes popping up in unlikely places around the garden.

Features: flowers; habit; foliage **Habit:** deciduous large shrub or small tree with arching branches **Height:** 4–20' **Spread:** 4–20' **Hardiness:** zones 4–8

Camellia

Camellia

Camellias tolerate salt and pollution, making them excellent choices for coastal urban plantings.

Growing

Camellias prefer to grow in **light shade** or **partial shade** in **well-drained, acidic to neutral** soil that is **high in organic matter**. Protect camellias from strong, hot sun and drying winds. They may also suffer damage if temperatures drop below 15° F.

Plant so the base of the tree is slightly above grade and soil is not covering the base. Use organic mulch to help keep the roots cool for the first two to three years.

Tips

Camellias are evergreen plants suitable for mixed beds, borders and woodland gardens, as specimens or as container plants. The soil for container plantings should be 50% organic matter and 50% potting mix.

Recommended

There are almost 300 species of camellias and thousands of cultivars. Check with your local nursery or garden center to see what is available.

Some camellias produce more flower buds than they can open. Selectively removing the buds allows the remaining buds to form larger, stronger flowers. If you forget, don't worry. Natural bud drop may be caused by overwatering, underwatering or a period of very low humidity.

Features: flowers; foliage; habit **Habit:** upright to spreading, evergreen shrub or small tree **Height:** 18"–20'; sometimes to 50' **Spread:** 3–12' **Hardiness:** zones 7–9

Cedar

Cedrus

C. atlantica 'Glauca Pendula' (above), *C. deodara* (below)

A mature cedar tree, with its towering form and elegant, layered, sweeping branches, is truly a magnificent sight to behold.

Growing

Cedars grow well in **full sun** or **partial shade**. The soil can be any type as long as it is **well drained**, but a **moist, loamy** soil of **average to high fertility** is preferable.

Tips

Cedars are very large trees, best suited to large properties.

Recommended

C. atlantica (atlas cedar, blue atlas cedar) is a large, wide-spreading, pyramidal tree with branches that sweep the ground. Smaller cultivars are available. **'Glauca Pendula'** is an interesting cultivar with trailing branches.

C. deodara (deodar cedar) is the largest and fastest-growing cedar, but it is not very cold hardy. Cultivars more reasonable in size are often more tolerant of winter cold.

*Do not confuse the true cedars (*Cedrus*) with the native arborvitae (*Thuja*), which we commonly refer to as cedar.*

Features: habit; foliage; cones; bark **Habit:** large, upright, spreading or pendulous, evergreen tree **Height:** 3–130' **Spread:** 3–40' **Hardiness:** zones 5–8

Citrus

Citrus

Citrus trees provide a double benefit: they're attractive, and they produce wonderful fruit, including lemons, limes, grapefruits, oranges and kumquats.

Growing

Citrus prefer **full sun** and **well-drained** soil. Water infrequently but deeply; do not over water. When planting, position the root crown barely below the soil line. Mulch to keep soil cool and moist.

Tips

No matter where you live in California, there's a citrus tree that's just right for your garden. In cold winter areas, place a dwarf citrus in a pot and position it where it can benefit from reflected heat. Keep it on a wheeled platform and roll it to shelter when freezing temperatures arrive.

Recommended

***C. aurantifolia* 'Bearss Seedless Lime'** does well in cool areas and bears fruit year-round.

***C. limon* 'Eureka'** is a traditional lemon available as a dwarf that produces tasty, tart fruit year-round.

C. × *meyeri* (above), *C.* × *sinensis* 'Valencia' (below)

***C.* × *meyeri* 'Improved Meyer'** is a hardy cross between a lemon and Mandarin orange. It does not need as much heat as other varieties to bloom.

***C. paradisi* 'Oroblanco Grapefruit'** requires less heat than over varieties and produces sweet, seedless fruit in mid-winter.

***C.* × *sinensis* 'Valencia'** is a popular, juicy orange that holds fruit on the tree for long periods.

Citrus trees often drop blossoms because they produce more than the plants can support. This is natural. Because blossom drop can also be caused by overwatering, invest in a moisture meter.

Features: edible fruit; deep green foliage **Habit:** upright, evergreen tree **Height:** 8–22' **Spread:** 6–20' **Hardiness:** zones 8–10

Crepe Myrtle

Lagerstroemia

These flowering trees put on a great, long-lasting show in spring. Some varieties also deliver another spectacular display in fall when the leaves turn red. The smooth bark exfoliates throughout the year, revealing multicolored bark beneath.

L. indica (above & below)

Growing

Crepe myrtles prefer **full sun** with **average, well-drained** soil. They like deep but infrequent watering and perform best where a warm summer is followed by a cool fall.

Once trees are established, minimize fertilization—fertilizer encourages leaf growth at the expense of flowers. They bloom on new wood, so trim in winter or early spring.

Tips

Crepe myrtles can be used in a variety of ways—as tall, colorful standouts in a perennial bed, in a container to brighten a sunny courtyard, or in a row to define a property line.

Recommended

***L.* hybrids** are available in many colors and heights. Flower colors include white, pink, lavender, coral, red and everything in between. Use them as trees or shrubs. **'Acoma'** bears white, crinkled flowers over a long period. **'Arapaho'** has outstanding red, summer blossoms followed by brilliant maroon-tipped fall foliage. It is somewhat drought tolerant.

L. indica is a taller species (up to 25', though there are also dwarf versions) that flowers in shades of pink, red, purple or white. Many varieties feature leaves that change to red in fall. **'Catawba'** sports clusters of purple, spring flowers contrasting with bright green leaves.

Crepe myrtles are subject to powdery mildew in humid areas.

Also called: crape myrtle **Features:** bark; flowers; foliage **Habit:** multi-trunked, upright and open or weeping, deciduous tree **Height:** 3–30' **Spread:** 3–30' **Hardiness:** zones 7–9

Dawn Redwood

Metasequoia

Dawn redwood is a refined, pyramidal tree with attractive, deeply furrowed, cinnamon red, flaking bark. Don't worry when this ancient tree drops its needles—it's deciduous.

Growing

Dawn redwood grows well in **full sun** or **light shade.** The soil should be **humus rich,** slightly **acidic, moist** and **well drained**. It tolerates wet or dry soils, but growth rate is reduced in dry conditions. This tree likes humidity. Provide mulch and water regularly until it's established.

Tips

Dawn redwoods need plenty of room to grow. Large gardens can best accommodate them.

The lower branches must be left in place for the trunk to develop its characteristic buttress. Buttressed trunks are flared and grooved, and the branches appear to be growing from deep inside the grooves.

Recommended

M. glyptostroboides has a pyramidal, sometimes spire-like form. The needles turn gold or orange in fall before dropping. The cultivars are narrower than the species.

This tree is often called a "living fossil" because it was discovered in fossil form before it was found growing in China in the 1940s.

Dawn redwood is becoming a common sight in parks, golf courses and large gardens in North America.

Features: foliage; bark; cones; buttressed trunk **Habit:** narrow, conical, deciduous conifer **Height:** 70–125' **Spread:** 15–25' **Hardiness:** zones 5–8

Dogwood

Cornus

C. kousa (above & below)

The delicate branch patterns and spreading crowns of dogwood trees can add classic beauty to your garden.

Growing

Dogwoods grow well in **full sun, light shade** or **partial shade**, with a slight preference for light shade. The soil should be of **average to high fertility, high in organic matter, neutral to slightly acidic** and **well drained**.

Tips

Plant shrub dogwoods in groups in shrub or mixed borders. Tree species make wonderful specimens and are small enough to include in most gardens. Use them along the edge of a woodland garden, in a shrub or mixed border, alongside a house or near a pond, water feature or patio.

Features: late spring to early summer flowers; fall foliage; stem color; fruit; habit **Habit:** deciduous shrub or small tree **Height:** 5–40' **Spread:** 5–30' **Hardiness:** zones 2–8

Recommended

There are numerous dogwoods available. Small shrub species and their cultivars are tough plants, often grown for their bright red, orange or yellow stems that provide winter interest. The larger shrubs and trees bear inconspicuous flowers surrounded by showy white or pink bracts in spring or early summer. Some species have attractive horizontal branching, and some bear showy fruit. Many have attractive fall color. Check with your local garden center for availability.

C. kousa *is more dependable and disease resistant than many other dogwood species.*

Euonymus

Euonymus

E. alatus (above), *E. fortunei* (below)

Few plants can match the stunning fall color of burning bush, a popular euonymus variety. It can be used in many different landscape situations, as can wintercreeper euonymus.

Growing

Euonymus species prefer **full sun** but tolerate light shade or partial shade. Soil of **average to high fertility** is preferable, but any **moist, well-drained** soil will do.

The name Euonymus *means "of good name," an ironic translation given that all parts of these plants are poisonous and violently purgative.*

Tips

E. alatus can be grown in a shrub or mixed border, as a specimen, in a naturalistic garden or as a hedge. Dwarf cultivars can be used to create informal hedges.

Grow *E. fortunei* as a shrub in a border or as a hedge. It is an excellent substitute for the more demanding boxwood. The trailing habit also makes it useful as a groundcover or climber.

Recommended

E. alatus (burning bush, winged euonymus) is an attractive, open, mounding, deciduous shrub with corky ridges on the stems and branches and vivid red fall foliage. Cultivars are available.

E. fortunei (wintercreeper euonymus) is the parent plant of many attractive cultivars. It can be a prostrate, climbing or mounding evergreen, often with attractive, variegated foliage.

Features: foliage; corky stems (*E. alatus*); habit **Habit:** deciduous or evergreen shrub, small tree, groundcover or climber **Height:** 2–20' **Spread:** 2–20' **Hardiness:** zones 3–8

False Cypress

Chamaecyparis

Conifer shoppers have a marvelous selection of false cypresses that offer color, size, shape and growth habits not available in most other evergreens. False cypresses do best in the northern part of the state where they receive some winter chill.

Growing

False cypresses prefer **full sun**. The soil should be **fertile, moist, neutral to acidic** and **well drained**. Alkaline soils are tolerated. In shaded areas, growth may be sparse or thin.

Tips

Tree varieties are used as specimen plants and for hedging. The dwarf and slow-growing cultivars are used in borders and rock gardens and as bonsai. False cypress shrubs can be grown near the house or as evergreen specimens in large containers.

Features: foliage; habit; cones **Habit:** narrow, pyramidal, evergreen tree or shrub **Height:** 1–150' **Spread:** 1–65' **Hardiness:** zones 4–8

Recommended

There are several available species of false cypress, and many cultivars. The scaly foliage comes in a drooping or strand form, in fan-like or feathery sprays, and it may be dark green, bright green or yellow. Plant forms vary too, from mounding or rounded to tall and pyramidal or narrow with pendulous branches. Check with your local garden center to see what is available.

The oils in the foliage of false cypress may irritate sensitive skin.

Fothergilla

Fothergilla

F. major (above & below)

Foliage is a key element in a well-planned garden. Fothergilla has lovely gray-green leaves that stand out against evergreens in a woodland garden. It also boasts fiery fall foliage, which, along with fragrant flowers and interesting soft tan to brownish stems, give fothergilla year-round appeal. Fothergilla does best in northern California.

Growing

Fothergillas grow equally well in **full sun** or **partial shade**. Full sun will produce the most flowers and the best fall color. The soil should be of **average fertility, acidic, humus rich, moist** and **well drained**.

Tips

Fothergillas are attractive and useful in shrub or mixed borders, in woodland gardens and when combined with evergreen groundcover. Fothergillas look great paired with rhododendrons and azaleas.

Recommended

F. gardenii (dwarf fothergilla) is a bushy shrub that bears fragrant, white flowers. The foliage turns yellow, orange and red in fall. Cultivars are available.

F. major (large fothergilla) is a larger, rounded shrub that bears fragrant, white flowers. The fall colors are yellow, orange and scarlet. Cultivars are available.

Fothergilla's bottlebrush-shaped flowers have a delicate honey scent.

Features: spring flowers; scent; fall foliage **Habit:** dense, rounded or bushy, deciduous shrub **Height:** 2–10' **Spread:** 2–10' **Hardiness:** zones 4–8

Fringe Tree

Chionanthus

C. virginicus (above & below)

Cold-hardy fringe trees adapt to a wide range of growing conditions. They are densely covered in silky white, honey-scented flowers that shimmer in the wind for a long period in early summer.

Growing

Fringe trees prefer **full sun**. They do best in soil that is **fertile, acidic, moist** and **well drained**, but they will adapt to most soil conditions. Fringe trees prefer some winter chill.

Tips

Fringe trees work well as specimen plants, as part of a border or beside a water feature. Plants flower at a very early age.

Fruit from the fringe tree will attract birds to the garden, but if a tree lacks both female and male flowers, it will not produce fruit.

Recommended

C. retusus (Chinese fringe tree) is a rounded, spreading shrub or small tree with deeply furrowed, peeling bark and erect, fragrant, white flower clusters. (Zones 5–8)

C. virginicus (white fringe tree) is a spreading small tree or large shrub that bears drooping, fragrant, white flowers.

Fringe trees can be very difficult to find in general nurseries. Specialty nurseries and plant sales at botanical gardens, universities or colleges are the most likely places to find them.

Features: early-summer flowers; bark; habit **Habit:** rounded or spreading, deciduous large shrub or small tree **Height:** 10–25' **Spread:** 10–25' **Hardiness:** zones 4–8

Heather

Erica

E. carnea (above), 'Mediterranean Pink' (below)

Heathers come in so many forms with such varied flowering times that you can enjoy a textural tapestry of flowering heather in your garden almost year-round.

Growing

Heathers prefer **full sun** but tolerate partial shade. The soil should be of **average fertility, acidic, moist** and **well drained**. Although heathers prefer acidic soils and enjoy having peat moss mixed into the substrate, they will tolerate alkaline soil. Do not overfertilize.

Tips

Heathers make excellent groundcovers and rock garden plants. They can be combined with other acid-loving plants in a shrub or mixed border.

Recommended

E. carnea and its many available cultivars have flowers in several shades of pink, red, purple and white. Its foliage colors include yellow, orange, bronze and many shades of green.

***E.* × *darleyensis* 'Mediterranean Pink'** is a common mounding groundcover that bears rose-lavender flowers.

Bees are attracted to heather and produce a dark, richly flavored honey from its nectar.

Also called: spring heath, winter heath **Features:** late winter to mid-spring flowers; foliage; habit **Habit:** low, spreading, evergreen shrub **Height:** 6–12" **Spread:** 8–36" **Hardiness:** zones 5–7

Hibiscus

Hibiscus

H. rosa-sinensis (above), *H. syriacus* (below)

Stunning, delicate blossoms appear reliably on tall, attractive plants. Blooms last only a day, but the plants flower over a long period and attract hummingbirds and butterflies.

Growing

Hibiscus prefers **full sun** except in the hottest areas, where it will do well in partial shade. Plant in **enriched, well-drained** soil and provide regular water. Pinch back to encourage bushiness and repeat blooming.

Tips

Hibiscus is a dramatic plant that needs room to show off its glory. If used near a building, position it so it receives good air circulation to minimize mildew. Hibiscus can also be grown in large containers.

Recommended

H. rosa-sinensis is a tropical evergreen shrub that grows 4–8' tall, depending on the variety. It is available with single or double blooms in white, yellow, pink, rose, red or coral. Many varieties bloom spring through fall. **'C'est Bon'** bears huge, white-rimmed pink flowers from summer through fall. **'Copper Queen'** has attractive, dark foliage, but the real stars are the 11" flowers that open pink then change to white with a raspberry center and veins that radiate to the edge of each petal. **'Picante'** bears 6–8" flowers that are a spicy mixture of yellow, orange and red.

H. syriacus (rose of Sharon) is an upright, deciduous shrub that blooms from summer until frost. It bears 2–4" flowers in shades of red, pink, violet and purple.

If you see white flies fluttering about or notice cottony webs, blast the underside of the leaves with water every week.

Features: slender branches; foliage; flowers **Habit:** upright, evergreen or deciduous shrub **Height:** 4–10' **Spread:** 3–5' **Hardiness:** zones 6–11

Hydrangea

Hydrangea

H. macrophylla (above & below)

Hydrangeas have many attractive qualities including showy flowers and glossy, green leaves, some of which turn beautiful colors in fall.

Growing

Hydrangeas grow well in **full sun** or **partial shade**, and some species tolerate full shade. Shade or partial shade will reduce leaf and flower scorch in hotter regions. The soil should be of **average to high fertility, humus rich, moist** and **well drained**. These plants perform best in cool, moist conditions.

In many varieties, acidic soil will produce blue flowers, and alkaline soil will produce pink or red blooms.

Tips

Use hydrangeas in shrub or mixed borders, as specimens or informal barriers and in containers. Climbing hydrangea can be trained up walls, pergolas and arbors.

Recommended

H. arborescens (smooth hydrangea) is a rounded shrub that flowers well even in shade.

H. macrophylla (bigleaf hydrangea) is a rounded or mounding shrub. Many cultivars are available. (Zones 6–8)

H. paniculata (panicle hydrangea) is a large, spreading to upright shrub or small tree. **'Grandiflora'** (peegee hydrangea) is commonly available. (Zones 4–8)

H. quercifolia (oakleaf hydrangea) is a mound-forming shrub with attractive, exfoliating bark and large, oak-like leaves. (Zones 4–8)

Features: flowers; habit; foliage; bark **Habit:** mounding or spreading, deciduous shrub or tree **Height:** 3–80' **Spread:** 2–20' **Hardiness:** zones 3–8

Italian Cypress

Cupressus

Italian cypresses are wonderful trees that work well as hedges and screens.

Growing

Italian cypress prefers **full sun** in **well-drained** soil in a spot that has **shelter** from cold wind. It does well in heat and drier soil. Most Italian cypresses require little or no water after the second year.

Italian cypress doesn't usually require pruning. If growing Italian cypress as a hedge, begin training when the plant is young and trim only the young growth. Remove shoots that veer off in the wrong direction.

Tips

All Italian cypresses are long lived and make excellent specimen trees. They are also used as screens, windbreaks, hedges and boulevard trees.

Recommended

C. sempervirens is either narrowly columnar with upright branches or conical with horizontal branches. Both forms grow to 70' tall, and the horizontal branching form spreads to 20'. Both bear dense sprays of gray-green to dark green foliage. **'Tiny Tower'** ('Monshelby') is a unique, compact form with very dense foliage that grows 8' tall and 2' wide in 10 years. Mature size is estimated at 25–30' tall and 6–8' wide.

A unique feature of cypress is the mature bark that often breaks off into curling or rounded scales.

Also called: Mediterranean cypress, funeral cypress **Features:** foliage; habit; bark; cones **Habit:** columnar to conical, evergreen tree **Height:** 20–70' **Spread:** 3–20' **Hardiness:** zones 7–10

Juniper

Juniperus

J. squamata (above), *J. conferta* (below)

The prickly foliage may give some gardeners a rash.

Junipers are tough and versatile. A form, color and texture is available for most landscaping situations.

Growing

Junipers prefer **full sun** but tolerate light shade. The soil should be of **average fertility** and **well drained**, but these plants tolerate most conditions.

Tips

Junipers make prickly barriers, hedges and windbreaks. They can be used in borders, as specimens or in groups. The low-growing species can be used in rock gardens and as groundcover. For interesting evergreen color, mix the yellow-foliaged junipers with blue-needled varieties.

Recommended

Junipers vary from species to species and often from cultivar to cultivar within a species. ***J. chinensis*** (Chinese juniper) is a conical tree or spreading shrub. ***J. conferta*** (shore juniper) is a bushy, prostrate shrub. ***J. horizontalis*** (creeping juniper) is a prostrate, creeping groundcover. ***J. procumbens*** (Japanese garden juniper) is a wide-spreading, low shrub. ***J. sabina*** (savin juniper) is a spreading to erect shrub. ***J. scopulorum*** (Rocky Mountain juniper) can be upright, rounded, weeping or spreading. ***J. squamata*** (singleseed juniper) forms a prostrate or low, spreading shrub or a small, upright tree.

Features: foliage; variety of color, size and habit **Habit:** conical or columnar tree, rounded or spreading shrub or prostrate groundcover; evergreen **Height:** 6"–70' **Spread:** 12"–25' **Hardiness:** zones 3–8

Katsura-Tree

Cercidiphyllum

The Katsura-tree is a classic tree that adds distinction and grace to the garden. Even in youth it is poised and elegant, ready to become a bewitching mature specimen.

Growing

Katsura-tree grows equally well in **full sun** or **partial shade**. The soil should be **fertile, humus rich, neutral to acidic, moist** and **well drained**. This tree will become established more quickly if watered regularly during dry spells for the first year or two.

Tips

Katsura-tree works well as a specimen or shade tree. The species is quite large and is best used in large gardens. The cultivar 'Pendula' is quite wide spreading but can be used in smaller gardens.

Recommended

C. japonicum is a slow-growing tree with heart-shaped, blue-green foliage that turns yellow and orange in fall and develops a spicy scent. **'Pendula,'** one of the most elegant weeping trees available, is usually grafted to a standard. Its mounding, cascading branches give the entire tree the appearance of a waterfall tumbling over rocks.

'Pendula' (above), *C. japonicum* (below)

This tree is native to eastern Asia, and the delicate foliage blends well into Japanese-style gardens.

Features: summer and fall foliage; habit **Habit:** rounded or spreading, often multi-stemmed, deciduous tree **Height:** 10–70' **Spread:** 10–70' **Hardiness:** zones 4–8

Lilac

Syringa

S. meyeri (above), *S. vulgaris* (below)

The hardest thing about growing lilacs is choosing from the many species and hundreds of cultivars available. Many need chilly weather for best performance, but some new varieties will also bloom in warmer areas.

Growing

Lilacs grow best in **full sun**. The soil should be **fertile, humus rich** and **well drained**. These plants tolerate open, windy locations. Give them space to avoid powdery mildew. Lilacs are hardy and will do well in cold areas.

Control growth by pinching; heavy pruning will reduce growth the following year.

Tips

Include lilacs in a shrub or mixed border, or use them to create an informal hedge. Japanese tree lilac can be used as a specimen tree.

Recommended

The following is a severely shortened list of really good lilacs. Check with your garden center to see what is available.

S. meyeri (Meyer lilac) is a compact, rounded shrub that bears fragrant, pink or lavender flowers. (Zones 3–7)

S. microphylla (littleleaf lilac) is an upright, broad-spreading shrub with small, tidy leaves and attractive, airy clusters of fragrant, lilac pink flowers. (Zones 4–8)

S. patula (Manchurian lilac) is a hardy lilac with few suckers and small clusters of fragrant, lilac-colored flowers. **'Miss Kim'** is denser in habit. Its dark green leaves turn burgundy in fall. (Zones 3–8)

S. vulgaris (French lilac, common lilac) is a suckering, spreading shrub with an irregular habit and fragrant, lilac-colored flowers. It is a good selection for low-chill areas.

Features: late spring to midsummer flowers; habit **Habit:** rounded or suckering, deciduous shrub or small tree **Height:** 4–20' **Spread:** 4–20' **Hardiness:** zones 3–9

Magnolia

Magnolia

M. × soulangeana (above & below)

Magnolias are beautiful, fragrant, versatile plants that also provide attractive winter structure.

Growing

Magnolias grow well in **full sun** or **partial shade**. The soil should be **fertile, humus rich, acidic, moist** and **well drained**. A summer mulch will help keep the roots cool and the soil moist.

Avoid planting magnolias where the morning sun will encourage the blooms to open too early in the season. Cold, wind and rain can damage the blossoms.

Tips

Magnolias are used as specimen trees, and the smaller species can be used in borders.

If your garden center doesn't stock a good selection of magnolias, consider a mail-order source.

Recommended

Many species, hybrids and cultivars, in a range of sizes and with differing flowering times and flower colors, are available. Check with your local garden center.

M. grandiflora (southern magnolia) is a large, dense, broad, pyramidal evergreen tree. Its spectacular, fragrant blooms have inspired poets and artists for generations.

M. × soulangeana (saucer magnolia) is a rounded, spreading, deciduous shrub or tree with pink, purple or white flowers.

M. stellata (star magnolia) is a compact, bushy or spreading, deciduous shrub or small tree with many-petaled, fragrant, white flowers.

Features: flowers; fruit; foliage; habit; bark **Habit:** upright to spreading, deciduous or evergreen shrub or tree **Height:** 10–60' **Spread:** 10–50' **Hardiness:** zones 3–8

Maple

Acer

A. palmatum (above & below)

Maples are attractive year-round, with delicate flowers in spring, beautiful foliage and hanging samaras in summer, vibrant leaf color in fall and interesting bark and branch structures in winter.

Growing

Generally, maples do well in **full sun** or **light shade**, though light preferences vary from species to species. The soil should be **fertile, moist, rich in organic matter** and **well drained**.

Tips

Use maples as specimen, shade or street trees, as large elements in shrub or mixed borders or as hedges. Some are useful as understory plants bordering wooded areas; others can be grown in containers on patios or terraces.

A Japanese garden is not complete without attractive, smaller maples. Almost all maples can be used to create bonsai specimens.

Recommended

Many maples grow very large, but smaller species that suit small gardens exist, including ***A. circinatum*** (vine maple, Oregon vine maple), ***A. ginnala*** (amur maple), ***A. japonicum*** (full-moon maple, Japanese maple), ***A. palmatum*** (Japanese maple) and ***A. rubrum*** (red maple). Check with your local garden center for availability.

The red maple (A. rubrum) *is one of the few ornamental trees that will thrive in deep shade.*

Features: foliage; bark; winged fruit (samaras); fall color; habit; flowers **Habit:** small, multi-stemmed, deciduous tree or large shrub **Height:** 6–50' **Spread:** 10–40' **Hardiness:** zones 2–8

Pine

Pinus

P. mugo (above), *P. strobus* (below)

Pines offer exciting possibilities for any garden. Exotic-looking pines are available with soft or stiff needles, needles with yellow bands, trunks with patterned or mother-of-pearl–like bark and varied forms.

Growing

Pines grow best in **full sun**. These trees adapt to most **well-drained** soils but do not tolerate polluted urban conditions. These trees are not heavy feeders; fertilizing will encourage rapid new growth that is weak and susceptible to pest and disease problems.

To keep low-growing pines compact, pinch up to half of the new growth each spring.

Tips

Pines can be used as specimen trees, as hedges or to create windbreaks. Smaller cultivars can be included in shrub or mixed borders.

Recommended

There are many available pines, both trees and shrubby dwarf plants. Check with your local garden center or nursery to find out what is available.

The Austrian pine, P. nigra*, was often recommended as the most urban-tolerant pine, but overplanting has produced severe disease problems in this species, some of which can kill a tree in a single growing season.*

Features: foliage; bark; cones; habit **Habit:** upright, columnar or spreading, evergreen tree **Height:** 8–130' **Spread:** 15–60' **Hardiness:** zones 2–8

Pittosporum

Pittosporum

P. tenuifolium 'Marjorie Channon' (above & below)

The foliage of these evergreens forms an attractive background for other plants.

Growing

Pittosporum prefers **full sun** or **light shade** in **well-drained** soil. Give it regular water, though it will tolerate less water once established.

Thin out branches periodically to maintain form.

Tips

The tree form has an open, airy habit and works well in a border, as a screen or as a specimen plant when some height is needed. The shrub form can be used as a groundcover, foundation plant or in a mixed border.

Recommended

***P. tenuifolium* 'Marjorie Channon'** grows about 8' feet tall with an equal spread and features wide, green leaves with white borders. **'Silver Sheen'** has dark stems that contrast beautifully with the small, silvery leaves. This New Zealand tree can grow 15–25' tall.

P. tobira is a good hedge shrub or small tree with dark leaves and white, spring flowers that smell like orange blossoms. **'Wheelers Dwarf'** and **'Variegated Wheelers Dwarf'** are reliable and commonly available. For smaller spaces, consider **'Cream de Mint,'** with white-bordered, mint green leaves.

Pittosporum may attract aphids and scale, particularly when stressed. Provide consistent water.

Features: foliage; habit **Habit:** open, airy tree or dense, rounded shrub; evergreen **Height:** 6–25' **Spread:** 6–15' **Hardiness:** zones 8–11

Plumbago

Plumbago

These carefree, blowsy shrubs bear blue or white flowers over a long season. Plant one and your friends will be asking, "What is that?" Plumbagos do well in warmer parts of the state.

Growing

Plumbago does well in either **full sun** or **light shade**. Plant in **well-drained** soil and provide regular water until it is established.

Plumbago is evergreen in all but areas of hard frost. Trim it back in winter to keep it shapely.

Tips

Plumbago can be used as a foundation plant or as part of a mixed border.

Recommended

P. auriculata grows up to 6' tall as a shrub, or up to 12' tall when trained as a vine. Blossoms may be white, light blue or dark blue. **'Alba'** is a reliable white variety. **'Imperial Blue'** and **'Royal Cape'** are attractive blue selections.

Blue plumbagos look particularly attractive against a white fence.

Also called: cape leadwort, cape plumbago **Features:** habit; flowers **Habit:** sprawling, evergreen to semi-evergreen shrub **Height:** 6'; up to 12' if grown as a vine **Spread:** 8–10' **Hardiness:** zones 8–11

Rhododendron • Azalea

Rhododendron

These beautiful plants are particularly popular in the northern part of the state, where filtered shade and humidity provide ideal growing conditions.

Growing

Rhododendrons prefer **partial shade** or **light shade**. Some will tolerate full sun in cooler areas. A location **sheltered** from strong winds is preferable. The soil should be **fertile, humus rich, acidic, moist** and very **well drained**. Rhododendrons are sensitive to high pH, salinity and winter injury. Mulch to keep the shallow roots cool.

Tips

Use rhododendrons and azaleas in shrub or mixed borders, in woodland gardens, as specimen plants, in group plantings, as hedges and informal barriers, in rock gardens or in planters on a shady patio or balcony.

Recommended

***R.* 'California Sunset'** from Monrovia is evergreen with variegated pink and white double blossoms.

Rhododendrons and azaleas are generally grouped together. Extensive breeding and hybridizing makes it more and more difficult to label them separately. Check with your local nursery to find out what other types do well in your area.

Weevils often make notches along the leaf margins of rhododendrons. The variety 'PJM' is resistant to these insects.

Features: late winter to early summer flowers; foliage; habit **Habit:** upright, mounding, rounded, evergreen or deciduous shrub **Height:** 2–12' **Spread:** 2–12' **Hardiness:** zones 3–8

Rockrose

Cistus

C. × *purpureus* (above), *C.* species (below)

Lovely crepe-paper flowers last only one day, but the plant will bloom repeatedly during spring and summer. Even out of bloom, the rounded shape and soft green leaves make it an attractive garden plant.

Growing

Rockrose prefers **full sun**, though it appreciates some afternoon shade. Plant in **average to poor** soil. It is drought tolerant and needs little water.

This shrub prefers a gentle trim rather than a hard pruning.

Tips

Rockrose is an evergreen favorite in low-water gardens. It is attractive in rock gardens and can be used as an informal hedge.

Also called: rock rose **Features:** foliage; flowers **Habit:** bushy or tall, evergreen shrub **Height:** 3–6' **Spread:** 3–6' **Hardiness:** zones 6–9

Recommended

C. albidus has white-gray leaves. Pink flowers may bloom in spring and summer.

C. × purpureus (orchid rockrose) grows about 4' tall and features reddish purple flowers with a red spot at the base of each petal. This hardy plant stands up well to a variety of conditions, including cool winds, hot sun, poor soil and limited water.

This Mediterranean native can be used as a firescaping plant in fire-prone areas. It will help slow the spread of fire as it approaches buildings.

Smokebush

Cotinus

'Royal Purple' (above & below)

Try encouraging a clematis vine to wind its way through the spreading branches of a smokebush.

Bright fall color, adaptability, flowers of differing colors and variable plant sizes and forms make smokebush and all its cultivars excellent additions to the garden.

Growing

Smokebush grows well in **full sun** or **partial shade**. It prefers soil of **average fertility** that is **well drained**, but it will adapt to all but very wet soils.

Tips

Smokebush can be used in a shrub or mixed border, as a single specimen or in groups. It is a good choice for a rocky hillside planting.

Recommended

C. coggygria is a bushy, rounded shrub with large, puffy plumes of flowers that start out green and gradually turn a pinky gray. The green foliage turns red, orange or yellow in fall. Many cultivars are available, including purple-leaved varieties. **'Flame'** develops into a small, bushy tree or large shrub with purple-pink plumes and brilliant red fall color. **'Royal Purple'** has dark purple foliage and purple-gray flowers.

Also called: smoketree **Features:** early summer flowers; summer and fall foliage **Habit:** bushy, rounded, spreading, deciduous tree or shrub **Height:** 10–20' **Spread:** 10–15' **Hardiness:** zones 4–8

Spruce

Picea

P. abies (above), *P. pungens* (below)

The spruce is one of the most commonly grown and commonly abused evergreens. Plant spruces where they have enough room to spread, then let them branch all the way to the ground.

Growing

Spruce trees grow best in **full sun**. The soil should be **deep, moist, well drained** and **neutral to acidic**. These trees generally do not like hot, dry or polluted conditions. Spruce does not do well in heat; plant where summers are cool.

Spruces are best grown from small, young stock because they dislike being transplanted after they mature.

Tips

Spruces are used as specimen trees. The dwarf and slow-growing cultivars can also be used in shrub or mixed borders. These trees look most attractive when allowed to keep their lower branches.

Recommended

Spruces are generally upright, pyramidal trees, but cultivars may be low growing, wide spreading or even weeping in habit. ***P. abies*** (Norway spruce), ***P. breweriana*** (weeping spruce, Brewer spruce), ***P. glauca*** (white spruce), ***P. omorika*** (Serbian spruce), ***P. pungens*** (Colorado spruce) and their cultivars are popular and commonly available. The most common spruce for home landscaping is the cone-shaped ***P. glauca* var. *albertiana* 'Conica'** (dwarf Alberta spruce), a slow-growing specimen shrub.

Oil-based pesticides such as dormant oil can take the blue out of your blue-needled spruces.

Features: foliage; cones; habit **Habit:** conical or columnar, evergreen tree or shrub **Height:** 3–80' **Spread:** 3–25' **Hardiness:** zones 2–8

Stewartia

Stewartia

S. *monadelpha* (above & below)

Stewartias are wonderful plants that provide year-round interest. Plant them in areas such as the front yard or near a patio where their large, white, summer blooms, brilliant fall color and exfoliating bark, which peels or flakes, will be most appreciated.

Growing

Stewartias grow well in **full sun** or **light shade**. The soil should be of **average to high fertility, humus rich, neutral to acidic, moist** and **well drained**. These plants need some **shelter** from strong winds.

Plant only very young trees because stewartias do not transplant easily.

Tips

Plant stewartias as specimen trees and in groups. They make good companions for rhododendrons and azaleas because they enjoy the same growing conditions.

Recommended

S. monadelpha (tall stewartia) can be a shrubby, multi-stemmed tree or a narrowly conical, single-stemmed tree.

S. pseudocamellia (Japanese stewartia) is a broad, columnar or pyramidal tree.

Don't be concerned if the bark doesn't put on a display when you first plant a stewartia. It can take several years for the bark to flake. Branches less than 2" in diameter don't exfoliate.

Features: midsummer flowers; summer and fall foliage; exfoliating bark **Habit:** broad, conical or rounded, deciduous tree **Height:** 20–80' **Spread:** 20–40' **Hardiness:** zones 5–8

Viburnum

Viburnum

V. plicatum var. *tomentosum* (above & below)

Good fall color, attractive form, shade tolerance, scented flowers and attractive fruit put the viburnums in a class by themselves.

Growing

Viburnums grow well in **full sun, partial shade** or **light shade**. The soil should be of **average fertility, moist** and **well drained**. Viburnums tolerate both alkaline and acidic soils.

Tips

Viburnums can be used in borders and woodland gardens. They are a good choice for plantings near swimming pools.

Recommended

Many viburnum species, hybrids and cultivars are available. Hardiness varies among species. Some popular choices include ***V. carlesii*** (Korean spice viburnum), a dense, bushy, rounded, deciduous shrub with white or pink, spicy-scented flowers; ***V. plicatum* var. *tomentosum*** (doublefile viburnum), with lacy-looking, white flower clusters and graceful, horizontal branches that give the shrub a layered effect; ***V. trilobum*** (American cranberrybush, highbush cranberry), a dense, rounded shrub with clusters of white flowers followed by edible, red fruit; and ***V. tinus* 'Spring Bouquet,'** a dense, compact shrub with clusters of white flowers and persistent blue fruit that ripens to black.

Deadheading will keep these plants looking neat, but it will also prevent fruits from forming.

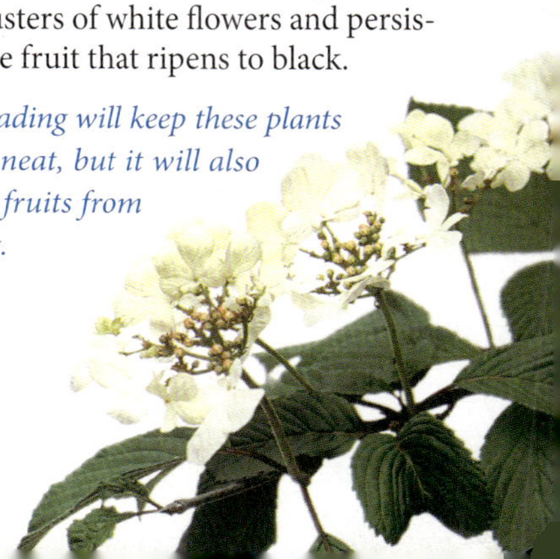

Features: flowers (some fragrant); summer and fall foliage; fruit; habit **Habit:** bushy or spreading, evergreen, semi-evergreen or deciduous shrub **Height:** 2–15' **Spread:** 2–15' **Hardiness:** zones 2–8

Weigela

Weigela

'Polka' (above), *W. florida* (below)

Weigelas have been improved through breeding, and specimens with more compact forms, longer flowering periods and greater cold tolerance are now available.

Growing

Weigelas prefer **full sun** but tolerate partial shade. The soil should be **fertile** and **well drained**. These plants will adapt to most well-drained soil conditions.

Tips

Weigelas can be used in shrub or mixed borders, in open woodland gardens and as informal barrier plantings.

Recommended

W. florida is a spreading shrub with arching branches that bears clusters of dark pink flowers. Many hybrids and cultivars are available, including dwarf varieties, red-, pink- or white-flowered varieties and varieties with purple, bronze or yellow foliage. The following are some newer selections: **'French Lace'** ('Brigela') has lime green to yellow leaf margins and dark, reddish pink flowers. **'Midnight Wine'** ('Elvera') is a dwarf plant with purple foliage and pink flowers. **'Wine and Roses'** ('Alexandra') has dark purple foliage and vivid pink flowers.

Weigela is one of the longest-blooming shrubs, with its main flush of blooms lasting as long as six weeks. It often re-blooms if sheared lightly after the first flowers fade.

Features: late spring to early summer flowers; foliage; habit **Habit:** upright or low, spreading, deciduous shrub **Height:** 1–9' **Spread:** 1–12' **Hardiness:** zones 3–8

Witch-Hazel

Hamamelis

H. virginiana (above & below)

Witch-hazels are wonderful four-season plants. They bloom in mid- to late winter, the flowers last for weeks, and their spicy fragrance awakens the senses.

Growing

Witch-hazel grows best in a **sheltered** location with **full sun** or **light shade**. The soil should be of **average fertility, neutral to acidic, moist** and **well drained**. Witch-hazel does better in cool areas, so enjoy it in the northern part of the state.

Tips

Witch-hazels work well individually or in groups. Plant them as specimen plants, in shrub or mixed borders or in woodland gardens. As small trees, they are ideal for small gardens.

Features: fragrant, early spring flowers; summer and fall foliage; habit **Habit:** spreading, deciduous shrub or small tree **Height:** 10–20' **Spread:** 10–20' **Hardiness:** zones 5–8

Recommended

H. × intermedia is a vase-shaped, spreading shrub that bears yellow, orange or red flowers and provides orange, red and bronze fall color.

H. japonica (Japanese witch-hazel) is an open, wide-spreading tree with yellow flowers, yellow fall color and attractive criss-crossed branches.

H. mollis (Chinese witch-hazel) is a dense, rounded, spreading shrub with zig-zagged branches, very fragrant, yellow flowers and orange or yellow fall color.

H. virginiana (common witch-hazel) is an erect tree with yellow fall foliage and flowers.

In cold weather, the petals roll up to protect the flowers and extend the flowering season.

Yucca

Yucca

'Golden Sword' (above), *Y. filamentosa* (below)

Yucca will add a touch of the desert to your personal oasis.

Growing

Yucca grows best in **full sun**. Any **well-drained** soil is suitable. This drought-tolerant plant grows best in areas of low humidity.

Pruning is not needed, but the flower spikes can be removed when flowering is finished, and dead leaves can be removed as needed.

Tips

This spiky plant looks as though it belongs in a desert or a southern garden. As a specimen in pots, planters and urns, yucca makes a strong architectural statement. The variegated varieties add color and texture to beds and borders.

Recommended

Y. filamentosa has long, stiff, finely serrated, pointed leaves with threads that peel back from the edges. It is the most frost-hardy yucca species available. **'Bright Edge'** has leaves with yellow margins. **'Golden Sword'** has leaves with yellow centers and green margins. **'Hofer's Blue'** has attractive, blue-green leaves and is salt tolerant.

The striking white flowers are edible raw or cooked and are said to taste like Belgian endive. Try adding them to a salad.

Also called: Adam's needle **Features:** summer flowers; foliage; habit **Habit:** rounded rosette of long, stiff, spiky, evergreen leaves **Height:** 24–36"; up to 6' in flower **Spread:** 24–36" **Hardiness:** zones 5–9

Abraham Darby

Modern Shrub Rose

Named after a British industrialist, the hard-working Abraham Darby rose lives up to its name with repeat, long-lasting blooms. Buy one when you can—this popular rose is frequently out of stock.

Growing

Abraham Darby prefers **full sun** with some shade in areas with very hot summers. Before planting, amend **fertile, moist, well-drained** soil with compost. Water deeply once a week during the growing season. To assist with repeat blooms, fertilize during the growing season.

Tips

Abraham Darby is an attractive shrub rose that works well as a foundation plant or in a mixed border, but it can also be trained as a short, 8' tall climber.

Recommended

Rosa **'Abraham Darby'** is a sturdy, fragrant rose that grows 5' tall with an equal spread. Double, cupped, fragrant, pink-tinged apricot flowers are borne throughout summer on a bushy shrub with an arching habit.

Abraham Darby does well in all areas of California and is prized for its fragrant blossoms and arching form.

Features: repeat blooming, summer flowers; fragrance; habit **Flower color:** apricot tinged with pink **Height:** 5–8' **Spread:** 5' **Hardiness:** zones 5–10

Bonica

Modern Shrub Rose

Bonica was the first modern shrub rose to be named an All-America Selection. The blooms have a light, sweet fragrance. Bright orange hips appear after the pink, double flowers fade.

Growing

Bonica prefers **full sun** and **fertile, moist, well-drained** soil with at least **5% organic matter** mixed in, but this disease-resistant, hardy rose tolerates shade and poor soils. It can tolerate light breezes, but keep it out of strong winds. Roses are heavy feeders and drinkers and do not like to share their root space with other plants.

Tips

Bonica suits just about any location. Rose growers recommend it for mixed beds, containers, hedges, cut-flower gardens or as a groundcover, standard or specimen.

This beautiful rose has maintained worldwide popularity since its introduction in 1982.

Recommended

***Rosa* 'Bonica'** is a tidy, spreading rose of modest size that blooms profusely throughout most of the growing season. It bears an abundance of semi-glossy, rich green foliage that is beautiful enough to stand on its own.

Also called: Bonica '82, Meidomonac, Demon, Bonica Meidiland **Features:** repeat blooming, summer to fall flowers; easy maintenance; colorful hips **Flower color:** medium pink **Height:** 3–5' **Spread:** 3–4' **Hardiness:** zones 4–9

Double Delight

Hybrid Tea Rose

Double Delight is aptly named; it delights with its strong, sweet, lightly spicy fragrance and its unique flower color. The fully double, high-centered flowers open cream with red edges and gradually darken to solid red. Heat intensifies the color.

Growing

Double Delight prefers **full sun** and **fertile, moist, well-drained** soil with at least **5% organic matter** mixed in. Roses can tolerate light breezes, but keep them out of strong winds. Double Delight is a heavy feeder and drinker, and it does not like to share its root space with other plants.

Blackspot can be a problem for Double Delight. Cool, wet weather can promote mildew.

Tips

It's not hard to find a place for this unique flower color in a bed or border. Plant it in a warm, dry location.

Recommended

***Rosa* 'Double Delight'** is an upright, irregularly branched plant with mid-green foliage. Its fragrance is unaffected by temperature, light or age.

Double Delight is a long-lasting cut flower and a good choice for competition and exhibition.

Also called: Andeli **Features:** repeat blooming, summer to fall flowers; flower color; fragrance **Flower color:** cream with carmine red edges **Height:** 3–4' **Spread:** 2–3' **Hardiness:** zones 6–9

Flower Carpet

Modern Shrub Rose

Flower Carpet is easy to grow and is popular with beginners and experts alike.

Growing

Flower Carpet prefers to grow in **full sun** in **fertile, moist, well-drained** soil with at least **5% organic matter** mixed in. Keep it out of strong winds, but light breezes are acceptable. Roses are heavy feeders and drinkers and do not like to share their root space with other plants.

Tips

Flower Carpet can be used as a groundcover or low hedge for a sunny location. Plant it in containers, mixed borders or beds.

Recommended

***Rosa* 'Flower Carpet'** is a vigorous, disease-resistant rose with abundant, shiny, bright green foliage. The flowers bloom later than most roses and are borne in large clusters, creating a dense, colorful carpet of flowers. In mild coastal climates, it can hold its leaves through winter.

A new color of Flower Carpet has been introduced almost every year since its original release, including white and a variety of pink shades. Watch for apple blossom, white, pink, red and coral.

Also called: Heidetraum, Noatraum, Emera, Blooming Carpet, Emera Pavement, Pink Flower Carpet **Features:** summer to early winter, repeat blooming flowers; easy to grow **Flower color:** deep, hot pink **Height:** 30–36" **Spread:** 3–4' **Hardiness:** zones 4–9

Fourth of July

Modern Climber

Bearing unusual red-and-white-striped flowers, Fourth of July is cause for celebration with repeat blooms, lovely fragrance and disease resistance.

Growing

Fourth of July prefers **full sun** in slightly **acidic, moist, well-drained** soil. Water deeply and thoroughly. Place it where it will get good air circulation and has room to grow up and out. Deadhead to encourage repeat blooms.

Tips

Include this short climber in your garden where you can enjoy the smell—just mind the thorns.

Features: repeat blooming, spring to fall flowers; fragrance **Flower color:** red and white striped **Height:** 10–15' **Spread:** 3' **Hardiness:** zones 5–9

Recommended

***Rosa* 'Fourth of July'** is a repeat-blooming climber that can grow 10–15' tall and bears double, 4–5" inch wide, red-and-white-striped blooms on a plant with attractive, shiny, bright green leaves.

When it was introduced in 1999, Fourth of July became the first climber to win the All-American Rose Selection (AARS) award in 23 years.

Gold Medal

Grandiflora Rose

Are you looking for a yellow rose to complement your other garden plants? A good investment is Gold Medal, a vigorous repeat bloomer with attractive, dark green foliage.

Gold Medal has some thorns, so watch out when pruning.

Growing

Gold Medal prefers **full sun** in **moist, well-drained** soil. Water thoroughly and deeply. Prune in early spring after danger of frost has passed.

Tips

Gold Medal is a good choice for urban areas because it tolerates some pollution. Consider it for landscapes near freeways in borders or parkways, or as a foundation plant.

Recommended

***Rosa* 'Gold Medal'** bears abundant, golden yellow flowers in clusters on 4–6' tall, bushy plants. Flowers start out with pink edges and may fade to cream. They make good cut flowers.

Features: repeat blooming, spring to fall flowers
Flower color: golden yellow **Height:** 4–6'
Spread: 4–6' **Hardiness:** zones 5–9

Gourmet Popcorn

Miniature Rose

Gourmet Popcorn bears cascading clusters of rounded, white, semi-double, honey-scented flowers with short stems.

Growing

Gourmet Popcorn prefers **full sun** and **fertile, moist, well-drained** soil with at least **5% organic matter** mixed in. It can tolerate light breezes, but keep it out of strong winds. Roses are heavy feeders and drinkers and do not like to share their root space with other plants.

Tips

Gourmet Popcorn looks stunning planted en masse or in pots, containers and hanging baskets. Plant this rose where its fragrance can be enjoyed—alongside pathways, under windows or next to a garden bench.

Recommended

***Rosa* 'Gourmet Popcorn'** is a vigorous, compact, cushion-like, rounded shrub with lush, dark green foliage. It is resistant to disease. In warmer regions, Gourmet Popcorn can grow up to twice its typical height, creating an impressive specimen with hundreds of flowers in bloom at a time.

Gourmet Popcorn won the Royal National Rose Society Trial Ground Certificate in 1995 and is frequently voted a favorite by rose growers.

Also called: Summer Snow **Features:** form; repeat blooming, abundant, summer to fall flowers **Flower color:** white **Height:** 18–24" **Spread:** 24" **Hardiness:** zones 4–9

Graham Thomas

David Austin Climbing Rose

The vigorous growth, double blossoms, arching canes and strong fragrance of Graham Thomas combine to make it one of the world's favorite roses.

Growing

Give Graham Thomas **full sun** and plant in **compost-enriched, average, well-drained** soil. Water deeply and thoroughly. Especially in warm areas, this vigorous plant benefits from pruning in early spring to maintain its form.

Tips

Plant Graham Thomas near a wall where it can ramble and climb and display several flushes of blooms.

Recommended

***Rosa* 'Graham Thomas'** climbs 8–12' tall and bears golden yellow, cupped flowers over a long period. The flowers have a spicy fragrance.

Graham Thomas was voted the World's Favorite Rose by the World Federation of Rose Societies (WFRS) in 2009.

Features: flowers; intense fragrance
Flower color: yellow **Height:** 8–12'
Spread: 5–8' **Hardiness:** zones 5–9

Henri Martin

Old Garden Rose

Henri Martin is known for its moss-covered stems and sepals that emit a subtle balsam scent. It bears clusters of camellia-like, semi-double to double, rich pinky red, sweetly fragrant blossoms that pale with age.

Growing

Henri Martin grows well in **full sun** and tolerates light shade. It prefers **fertile, moist, well-drained** soil with at least **5% organic matter** mixed in, but it tolerates hot, dry summers and poor soil. Roses tolerate light breezes, but keep them out of strong winds. They are heavy feeders and drinkers and do not like to share their root space with other plants.

Henri Martin may suffer some winter dieback in colder regions. Prune out any deadwood in spring.

Tips

Henri Martin's arching, flexible canes require support. It grows well on an obelisk, trellis, tripod or pergola.

Recommended

***Rosa* 'Henri Martin'** is a vigorous moss rose with graceful, arching branches and plentiful, disease-free, rough foliage.

Attractive, dark orange hips emerge after flowering and remain on the shrub well into winter.

Also called: Red Moss, Old Red Moss **Features:** profuse, non-repeating, midsummer flowers; colorful hips; fragrance; moss-covered stems and sepals **Flower color:** rich pinky red **Height:** 3–5' **Spread:** 4' **Hardiness:** zones 4–9

Hot Cocoa

Floribunda Rose

An unusually colored reddish brown rose with a bit of purple and orange mixed in, Hot Cocoa is a showstopper in the garden or the vase.

Growing

Plant Hot Cocoa in **full sun** in **moist, compost-enriched** soil. Mulch to keep the soil cool and moist.

Tips

Place Hot Cocoa near a path, where visitors will be able to appreciate its fragrance as they walk by.

Recommended

***Rosa* 'Hot Cocoa'** bears repeat blooming, ruffled blossoms 3.5" across with lovely fragrance on a 5' tall shrub. The flowers bloom from May to fall and are complemented by dark green, disease-resistant leaves. Hot Cocoa does well in the north and can also be grown to zone 9.

Hot Cocoa was an AARS selection for 2003.

Features: repeat blooming, spring to fall flowers; unusual color; strong fragrance **Flower color:** reddish brown tinged with purple and orange **Height:** 5' **Spread:** 5' **Hardiness:** zones 5–9

Iceberg

Floribunda Rose

There's a good reason Iceberg roses are often planted around parks, shops and office buildings. They are non-stop bloomers in temperate areas and perform well in most parts of California.

Growing

Iceberg prefers **full sun** but will also bloom in light shade. Plant in **fertile, moist, well-drained** soil. Provide regular water and mulch.

Tips

This bush full of exuberant white blossoms complements many kinds of garden plants in a border. It also performs well as a hedge.

Recommended

***Rosa* 'Iceberg'** offers repeat, double, white blooms spring through fall, and sometimes has a slight pink tinge to the blossoms. It looks wonderful in the garden and also provides beautiful cut flowers. It requires little in the way of fussy care and also has some disease resistance. In warmer regions it can grow up to 7' tall, but it usually tops out at 4'. Iceberg is also available in pink.

Iceberg has won many awards, including World's Favorite Rose in 1983.

Features: repeat blooming, double, spring to fall flowers; hardiness **Flower color:** white, sometimes pink-tinged **Height:** 4–7' **Spread:** 3–4' **Hardiness:** zones 5–10

Julia Child

Floribunda Rose

This AARS selection combines beauty, fragrance and disease resistance.

Growing

Julia Child prefers **full sun** in **fertile, moist, well-drained** soil. Give it regular water. Like many roses, Julia Child should be trimmed back in late winter for a flush of growth in spring.

Tips

Use this rose in the front of the border where you can enjoy the fragrance and long-lasting blooms.

Recommended

***Rosa* 'Julia Child'** is a lovely plant with abundant, showy, repeat blooming, yellow flowers from June through December. It grows about 3' tall and wide, though it may get rangier in warmer areas. This rose does well in a wide range of climates and is suitable for northern and southern California.

An appropriately rich butter-colored rose, this variety was personally chosen by chef Julia Child to carry her name.

Features: repeat blooming, summer to fall flowers; fragrance **Flower color:** butter yellow **Height:** 3' **Spread:** 3' **Hardiness:** zones 5–9

Mister Lincoln

Hybrid Tea Rose

A classic red rose, Mister Lincoln features deep, velvety flowers with strong fragrance on a tall, vigorous bush.

Mister Lincoln is a classic red rose with long-lasting blooms and lovely fragrance.

Growing

Mister Lincoln prefers **full sun** and **moist, well-drained** soil. It will tolerate some drought once established.

Tips

Plant Mister Lincoln where the velvety texture and fragrance of its flowers can be appreciated.

Recommended

***Rosa* 'Mister Lincoln'** blooms almost continually on bushes 3–5' tall. The large, strong-stemmed flowers are excellent as cut flowers.

Features: repeat blooming flowers; fragrance
Flower color: red **Height:** 3–5' **Spread:** 3–5'
Hardiness: zones 5–9

Mutabilis

Old Garden Rose

Mutabilis' vermilion buds give way to buff yellow flowers, which soon change from yellow to shades of pink and finally to deep crimson. This changing color palette is an unusual but desirable trait that will brighten the gloomiest site.

Growing

Roses prefer to grow in **full sun** and **fertile, moist, well-drained** soil with at least **5% organic matter** mixed in. Mutabilis tolerates shade but is not fond of cold wind. Roses are heavy feeders and drinkers and do not like to share their root space with other plants.

Mutabilis is Latin for "changing," possibly a reference to the changing color of the petals.

Tips

Mutabilis works best as a specimen, but it makes a wonderful informal hedge. Its dark foliage contrasts well with the lighter foliage on other plants.

Recommended

***Rosa* 'Mutabilis'** has soft, red stems and glossy, red-tinged, dark green foliage. Plant size and shape will vary depending on its location. Some people claim this rose can reach heights of 10–25'. Mutabilis requires very little maintenance.

Also called: Tipo Idéale, *R. chinensis mutabilis*, *R. odorata* 'Mutabilis,' Butterfly Rose **Features:** interesting, repeat blooming, midsummer flowers; disease-resistant foliage **Flower color:** yellow, then pink and crimson **Height:** 4–6' **Spread:** 3–5' **Hardiness:** zones 5–10

Pat Austin

English (Austin) Rose

Pat Austin introduced a new and vivid color combination: rich copper shades on the upper sides of the petals and pale yellow on the undersides. It is difficult to miss this exceptional color contrast as the fragrant flowers open and expand.

Growing

Pat Austin prefers **full sun** and **fertile, moist, well-drained** soil with at least **5% organic matter** mixed in. Light breezes are tolerable, but keep roses out of strong winds. Roses are heavy feeders and drinkers and do not like to share their root space with other plants.

Tips

Pat Austin blends beautifully into mixed shrub borders, informal beds or containers. It can also be trained as a short climber.

Recommended

***Rosa* 'Pat Austin'** is a vigorous, medium-sized, gracefully spreading plant. The semi-glossy, deep green foliage complements the large, open, deeply cupped, coppery flowers. The flowers have a sharp, fruity fragrance.

Pat Austin may be difficult to find, but it is well worth looking for.

Features: repeat blooming, summer to fall flowers; graceful form **Flower color:** coppery amber, yellow **Height:** 3' **Spread:** 4' **Hardiness:** zones 5–9

Peace

Hybrid Tea Rose

In 1976, Peace was the first rose to be selected World's Favorite Rose by the World Federation of Rose Societies.

Growing

Peace prefers to grow in **full sun** in **fertile, moist, well-drained** soil with at least **5% organic matter** mixed in. Keep it out of strong winds, but light breezes are acceptable. Roses are heavy feeders and drinkers and do not like to share their root space with other plants.

Tips

Peace is an ideal cut-flower variety. It is suitable for rose beds, hedges and borders and is considered one of the best varieties to grow as a standard. It is a little resentful of hard pruning but fares well with moderate pruning.

Recommended

Rosa 'Peace' is an upright grower with moderately thorny canes bearing large, shiny, dark green foliage and mild, fruity scented flowers. The yellow flower color can become pale if the location is too hot, while the pink flower color intensifies in heat.

Peace has a moderate level of disease resistance but is prone to blackspot in cooler climates. Its overall health has been compromised as a result of being cloned millions of times since its introduction in 1945.

Also called: Gloria Dei, Mme A. Meilland, Gioia, Beke, Fredsrosen **Features:** repeat blooming, summer to fall flowers; easy to grow **Flower color:** soft yellow; baby pink edges **Height:** 4–6' **Spread:** 3–4' **Hardiness:** zones 5–9

Sally Holmes

Hybrid Musk Rose

Need a standout, fragrant plant to cover an outbuilding or wall? Sally Holmes, winner of many awards, is your girl.

Growing

Sally Holmes prefers **full sun** but will tolerate some shade. Plant it in **fertile, moist, well-drained** soil. Provide regular water. Mulch to keep the roots cool.

Tips

This long-bloomer can be grown as a large bush or trained as a 12' climber that will ramble about.

Recommended

***Rosa* 'Sally Holmes'** is near ever-blooming in warmer areas with white, single blossoms tinged with pink or apricot. The nearly thornless rose resists disease. In warmer regions of California, Sally Holmes will grow much larger than the 5' × 5' generally assigned to it.

Both disease resistant and heat tolerant, Sally Holmes is a carefree choice when you want to cover an area or structure with flowers.

Features: repeat blooming flowers; disease resistance
Flower color: white tinged with pink or apricot
Height: 6–12' **Spread:** 5' **Hardiness:** zones 5–9

Sheila's Perfume

Floribunda Rose

Sheila's Perfume's showy, bicolored blooms have won several fragrance awards, including the Edland Fragrance Award and the Glasgow Fragrance Award.

Growing

Sheila's Perfume prefers **full sun** in **fertile, moist, well-drained** soil with at least **5% organic matter** mixed in. Roses can tolerate light breezes, but keep them out of strong winds. Roses are heavy feeders and drinkers and do not like to share their root space with other plants.

Tips

Sheila's Perfume bears a classically formed flower, making this plant ideal for cutting gardens, borders, hedges, mixed beds and containers.

Recommended

***Rosa* 'Sheila's Perfume'** is a compact, bushy plant that tends to spread throughout summer in warmer climates. It is vigorous, disease resistant and weatherproof, and has red-tinged, glossy, dark green foliage and fruit-scented flowers. An average of 20 petals, borne singly or in clusters, makes up each double flower.

The name 'Sheila's Perfume' reflects a combination of the hybridizer's wife's name and the plant's most outstanding quality.

Features: repeat blooming, summer to fall, fragrant flowers **Flower color:** pale yellow and light pink with dark pink edges **Height:** 30–42" **Spread:** 24" **Hardiness:** zones 5–11

The Fairy

Modern Shrub Rose

The Fairy is popular with both novice and experienced gardeners. It bears large clusters of dainty, soft pink, rosette-shaped, double flowers.

Growing

The Fairy grows well in **full sun** or **partial shade** in **fertile, moist, well-drained** soil with at least **5% organic matter** mixed in. It is prone to blackspot when planted in partial shade, but it will still bloom and the flower color will fade more slowly. Roses can tolerate light breezes, but keep them out of strong winds. These heavy feeders and drinkers do not like to share their root space with other plants.

Tips

This rose can be used in containers, as a groundcover, in mixed beds and borders, as a weeping standard, or left to trail over a low wall or embankment. It looks great massed or planted as low hedging. It also makes a beautiful cut flower.

Recommended

***Rosa* 'The Fairy'** is a compact, mounding plant with moderately prickly canes and glossy foliage. It is trouble free and moderately resistant to disease. It blooms continually until fall frost.

The Fairy doesn't just tolerate neglect—it prefers it.

Also called: Fairy, Feerie **Features:** repeat blooming, late summer to fall flowers; low maintenance **Flower color:** soft pink **Height:** 24" **Spread:** 24"–4' **Hardiness:** zones 4–9

Tournament of Roses

Grandiflora Rose

Tournament of Roses' double, high-centered flowers are borne in symmetrical clusters of three to six. Each flower has 35 to 40 petals and a light, spicy fragrance.

Growing

Tournament of Roses prefers **full sun** and **fertile, moist, well-drained** soil with at least **5% organic matter** mixed in. It can tolerate light breezes, but keep it out of strong winds. Roses are heavy feeders and drinkers and do not like to share their root space with other plants.

The name refers to the annual rose parade held in Pasadena. This rose was released for sale on the parade's centenary.

Tips

Tournament of Roses blends into mixed beds and borders and works well in hedges and group plantings.

This long-lasting cut flower is one of the best grandifloras for display and exhibition. Warm weather brings out the best flower color.

Recommended

***Rosa* 'Tournament of Roses'** is a moderately vigorous, upright plant with glossy, dark green foliage and abundant flowers in various shades of pink. It has excellent continuity of bloom.

Also called: Berkeley, Poesie **Features:** repeat blooming, summer to fall, double flowers; easy to grow **Flower color:** medium coral pink **Height:** 36" **Spread:** 36" **Hardiness:** zones 4–9

Black-Eyed Susan Vine

Thunbergia

Black-eyed Susan vine is a useful flowering vine with simple flowers that give it a cheerful, welcoming appearance.

T. alata (above & below)

Growing

Black-eyed Susan vines do well in **full sun, partial shade** or **light shade**. Grow them in **fertile, moist, well-drained** soil that is **rich in organic matter**. Black-eyed Susan vines are evergreen in warmer areas with temperate summers.

Tips

Black-eyed Susan vines can be trained to twine up and around fences, walls, trees and shrubs. They also look attractive trailing down from the top of a rock garden or rock wall or growing in mixed containers and hanging baskets.

Recommended

T. alata is a vigorous, twining climber. It bears yellow flowers, often with dark centers, in summer and fall. Cultivars with large flowers in yellow, orange, salmon, rose or white are available.

T. grandiflora (skyflower vine, blue trumpet vine) is less commonly available than *T. alata*. It tends to bloom late, in early to mid-fall. This twining climber bears stunning, pale violet-blue flowers. **'Alba'** has white flowers.

The blooms are trumpet shaped, with the dark centers forming a tube.

Features: twining habit; dark-centered flowers **Flower color:** yellow, orange, violet-blue, creamy white **Height:** 5' or more **Spread:** 5' or more **Hardiness:** tender perennial grown as an annual

Bougainvillea

Bougainvillea

Bougainvillea's color comes from the bracts surrounding the flowers. Many varieties have thorns, which makes it an effective barrier plant.

Each tiny flower is surrounded by three wavy, papery, colorful bracts; the flowers can completely cover the plant.

Growing

Bougainvillea prefers **full sun**. The soil should be **moist** and **well drained**, though this plant requires little care once established. In cold areas, bougainvillea can be overwintered indoors or treated as an annual. Elsewhere, it is a vigorous grower.

Bracts form on new wood, so go ahead and trim. Bougainvillea does not like having its roots disturbed, so take special care when transplanting.

Tips

Adaptable to a variety of situations, bougainvillea can be trained as a trailing spreader, standard or climbing vine. When used as a vine, it requires physical attachment to walls, arbors and so on.

Recommended

B. glabra is a tender, evergreen plant with semi-glossy leaves. Many varieties are available. Check with your local garden center for those that perform well in your area.

Features: colorful bracts; thorns **Habit:** woody, evergreen vine **Height:** 15–30' **Spread:** 15–30' **Hardiness:** zones 9–11

Clematis

Clematis

Clematis loves to grow up stumps, where its roots can feed on decaying stump roots. Planted on the north side of a stump, it will clamber to the sunny side. It also makes a wonderful companion for roses.

Growing

Clematis plants prefer **full sun** but tolerate partial shade. The soil should be **fertile, humus rich, moist** and **well drained**. Clematis vines are quite cold hardy but will fare best when protected from winter wind.

These vines prefer their roots to be cool. A thick layer of mulch or a planting of low, shade-providing perennials will protect the tender roots. The rootball should be planted about 2" beneath the soil surface.

Tips

Clematis vines climb up structures such as trellises, railings, fences and arbors. They can also grow over shrubs and up trees and can be used as groundcover.

Recommended

There are many species, hybrids and cultivars of clematis. The beautiful flowers come in a variety of shapes and colors. The flower forms, blooming times and sizes of the plants can vary. Check with your local garden center to see what is available.

There are so many species, hybrids and cultivars of clematis that it is possible to have one in bloom all season.

Features: twining habit; early to late summer flowers; decorative seedheads **Flower color:** blue, purple, pink, yellow, red, white **Height:** 10–17' or more **Spread:** 5' or more **Hardiness:** zones 3–8

Climbing Hydrangea

Hydrangea

A mature climbing hydrangea can cover an entire wall, and with its dark, glossy leaves and delicate, lacy flowers, it is quite possibly one of the most stunning climbing plants available.

Growing

Hydrangeas prefer **partial shade** or **light shade** but tolerate both full sun and full shade. The soil should be of **average to high fertility, humus rich, moist** and **well drained**. These plants perform best in cool, moist conditions, so be sure to mulch their roots.

Tips

Climbing hydrangea climbs up trees, walls, fences, pergolas and arbors. It clings to walls by means of aerial roots and therefore needs no support, just a somewhat textured surface such as cinder or cement blocks. It also grows over rocks, can be used as a groundcover and can be trained to form a small tree or shrub.

Recommended

H. anomala* subsp. *petiolaris (*H. petiolaris*) is a clinging vine with dark, glossy, green leaves that sometimes turn an attractive yellow in fall. For over a month in midsummer, the vine is covered with white, lacy-looking flowers, and the entire plant appears veiled in a lacy mist.

Climbing hydrangea will produce the most flowers when it is exposed to some direct sunlight each day.

Features: flowers; clinging habit; exfoliating bark **Flower color:** white **Height:** 50–80' **Spread:** 50–80' **Hardiness:** zones 4–8

Cup-and-Saucer Vine

Cobaea

Cup-and-saucer vine, a vigorous climber native to Mexico, produces frilly, purple flowers from spring until frost.

Growing

Cup-and-saucer vine prefers **full sun**. The soil should be **well drained** and of **average fertility**. This plant is fond of hot weather and will do best if planted in a sheltered site with southern exposure. Set the seeds on edge when planting them, and barely cover them with soil.

Tips

Grow this vine up a trellis, over an arbor or along a chain-link fence. Cup-and-saucer vine requires a sturdy support to climb. It uses grabbing hooks to climb, so it can't grow up a wall without something to grab. It can be trained to fill almost any space. In hanging baskets, the vine will climb the hanger and spill over the edges.

In cooler parts of California, these tender plants can be cut back a bit in fall and overwintered indoors. Plants grown in hanging baskets are easiest to move indoors.

Recommended

C. scandens is a vigorous climbing vine that may grow up to 40' tall in warmer areas of the state. The flowers that are creamy green when they open and mature to deep purple. **Var. *alba*** has white flowers.

Also called: cathedral bells **Features:** flowers; clinging habit; long blooming period **Flower color:** green changing to purple, white **Height:** 15–25'; sometimes up to 40' **Spread:** 15–25' **Hardiness:** zones 9–11

Grape

Vitis

V. vinifera (above & below)

The grape's ripe fruit can attract wasps.

The grape vine's bold foliage and colorful fruit provide substance and a feel of permanence and weight that many new gardens need. Some grapes are grown primarily for their ornamental leaves, others for their edible fruit.

Growing

Grapes prefer **full sun** or **partial shade**. The soil should be **moist** and **acidic**. These plants tolerate most soil conditions as long as the soil is **well drained**.

Tips

Grape vines can be trained to grow on almost any sturdy structure. They may need to be tied in place until the basic structure is established. Especially in warm areas, grapes grow fast. Make sure to choose a variety that's right for your region—there are many kinds available.

Recommended

V. coignetiae (crimson glory vine) is a woody climber with attractive, scarlet fall color. It bears inedible, small, dark purple fruit. (Zones 5–8)

V. rotundifolia (muscadine grape) bears purple or greenish purple fruit that is edible but bitter. Fall color is yellow. (Zones 5–8)

V. vinifera (wine grape) is an attractive, woody climber, best known for the wine grapes it produces. **'Purpurea'** is a good performer that bears deep purple foliage. (Zones 6–8)

Features: summer and fall foliage; late summer to fall fruit; habit **Habit:** woody, climbing, deciduous vine **Height:** 22–50' **Spread:** 22–50' **Hardiness:** zones 5–9

Hardenbergia

Hardenbergia

H. violacea (above), 'Happy Wanderer' (below)

An evergreen vine with a long bloom season, hardenbergia bears sweet pea–like flowers in an assortment of shades.

Growing

Hardenbergia prefers **full sun** except in hot areas, where it benefits from partial shade. Plant it in the ground or in a container in **well-drained** soil, and provide moderate water.

Tips

Hardenbergia climbs by twining stems, so provide a trellis or some other structure to enjoy its decorative flowers and foliage.

This Australian native looks delicate but is hardy in mild winter regions.

Also called: lilac vine **Features:** evergreen; foliage; flowers **Flower color:** violet, lilac, rose, white **Height:** 12–16' **Spread:** 12–24" **Hardiness:** zones 9–11

Recommended

H. comptoniana has lacy green foliage and light blue flowers. It looks good in or out of bloom.

H. violacea does not have as delicate foliage, but this species comes in a variety of colors including pink, white and purple. **'Happy Wanderer'** has pink blooms and is a hardy variety often found at retailers. **'Icicle'** has white blossoms. **'Meema,'** a dwarf version, has dark purple flowers.

Hardy Kiwi

Actinidia

A. arguta (above & below)

Hardy kiwi is handsome in its simplicity. This vine is grown for its lovely foliage.

Growing

Hardy kiwi vines grow best in **full sun** but tolerate partial shade. The soil should be **fertile** and **well drained**. These plants require shelter from strong winds. Cool weather brings out the best color. In warm areas, give it some shade.

Hardy kiwi vines can grow uncontrollably. Prune them back if they get out of hand.

Kiwi vines may take 10 years to mature to fruiting age.

Tips

These vines need a sturdy structure to twine around. Pergolas, arbors and sufficiently large and sturdy fences provide good support. Given a trellis against a wall, a tree or some other upright structure, hardy kiwis will twine upward all summer. They can also be grown in containers.

Recommended

A. arguta (hardy kiwi, bower actinidia) has dark green, heart-shaped leaves, white flowers and smooth-skinned, greenish yellow, edible fruit.

A. kolomikta (variegated kiwi vine, kolomikta actinidia) has green leaves strongly variegated with white and pink, white flowers and smooth-skinned, greenish yellow, edible fruit.

Also called: actinidia **Features:** early summer flowers; edible fruit; twining habit **Flower color:** white **Height:** 15–30' to indefinite **Spread:** 15–30' to indefinite **Hardiness:** zones 3–8

Honeysuckle

Lonicera

Honeysuckles can be rampant, twining vines, but with careful consideration and placement, they won't overrun your garden. The fragrance of the flowers makes any effort worthwhile.

'Dropmore Scarlet' (above & below)

Growing

Honeysuckles grow well in **full sun** or **partial shade**. The soil should be **average to fertile, humus rich, moist** and **well drained**.

Tips

Honeysuckle can be trained to grow up a trellis, fence, arbor or other structure. In a large container near a porch, it will ramble over the edges of the pot and up the railings with reckless abandon.

Recommended

Many cultivars and hybrids are available with flowers in yellow, red or scarlet, including ***L.* × *brownii* 'Dropmore Scarlet,'** one of the hardiest of the climbing honeysuckles, cold hardy to zone 4. It bears bright red flowers for most of summer.

L. caprifolium (Italian honeysuckle, Italian woodbine) bears fragrant, creamy white or yellow flowers in late spring and early summer.

L. sempervirens (trumpet honeysuckle, coral honeysuckle) bears orange or red flowers in late spring and early summer.

There are dozens more honeysuckle species, hybrids and cultivars. Check with your local garden center to see what is available.

Honeysuckle attracts hummingbirds and bees with its rich fragrance and nectar.

Features: late spring and early summer flowers; twining habit; fruit **Flower color:** orange, red, yellow, creamy white **Height:** 6–20' **Spread:** 6–20' **Hardiness:** zones 5–8

Passion Flower

Passiflora

Passion flower is a fast-growing, woody climber that is a perennial in warmer regions. It will thrive for years next to a house without any winter protection. The flowers are mesmerizing.

Growing

Grow passion flower in **full sun** or **partial shade**. This plant prefers **well-drained, moist** soil of **average fertility**. Keep it sheltered from wind and cold.

Fertilize passion flower sparingly. Too much nitrogen will encourage lots of foliage but few flowers. Thin it out during the growing season of late winter/early spring.

Tips

Passion flower is a popular addition to mixed containers and makes an unusual focal point near a door. The vines grow by tendrils, so give them something to twine around.

Recommended

P. caerulea (blue passion flower) is a vigorous climber that bears unusual, purple-banded, purple-white flowers all summer. **'Constance Elliott'** bears fragrant, white flowers.

Most passion flowers are native to South America.

Features: exotic flowers; habit; foliage **Flower color:** white or pale pink petals with blue or purple bands **Height:** up to 30' **Spread:** variable **Hardiness:** zones 6–8

Sweet Pea

Lathyrus

Sweet peas are among the most enchanting annuals. Their fragrance is intoxicating.

Growing

Sweet peas prefer **full sun** but tolerate light shade. The soil should be **fertile, rich in organic matter, moist** and **well drained**. The plants tolerate light frost. Fertilize very lightly during the flowering season.

Soak seeds in water for 24 hours or nick them with a nail file before planting. Plant a second crop of sweet peas about a month later to ensure a longer blooming period.

Deadheading also extends the blooming season. As soon as you allow blossoms to fade on the vine, it will stop flowering.

Tips

Sweet peas will grow up poles, trellises and fences or over rocks. They cling by wrapping tendrils around whatever they are growing up, so they do best when they have a rough surface, chain-link fence, small twigs or a net to cling to.

Recommended

There are many cultivars of ***L. odoratus***, including some that are small and bushy rather than climbing. Heritage varieties are often the most fragrant.

Avoid planting this vine in the same location two years in a row to help prevent some diseases from afflicting your sweet peas.

Features: clinging habit; summer flowers **Flower color:** pink, red, purple, lavender, blue, salmon, pale yellow, peach, white; also bicolored **Height:** 12"–6' **Spread:** 6–12" **Hardiness:** hardy annual

Trumpet Vine

Campsis

The dark, shiny leaves are attractive even when the plant is not covered in lovely, trumpet-shaped flowers in a variety of colors. In warmer areas, this evergreen vine requires minimal care.

Growing

Plant trumpet vine in **full sun** or **partial shade** in **well-drained** soil. Provide regular water until it is established.

Trumpet vine can take over your garden, so keep it in check with judicious pruning and pinching in late winter.

Tips

The vines spread by aerial rootlets that adhere to various surfaces. If you have a wall, fence or building you want to cover in a hurry, enlist the aid of a trumpet vine.

Recommended

C. × ***tagliabuena*** is a vigorous vine that can grow 30–40' tall. It is available in variety of flower colors including red, lavender, coral and white.

Trumpet vines have an invasive root system; put down a root barrier to avoid having trumpet vines throughout your neighborhood.

Also called: trumpet creeper **Features:** rapid growth; flowers **Flower color:** red, lavender, coral, white **Height:** 30–40' **Spread:** 15–20' **Hardiness:** zones 4–9

Virginia Creeper

Parthenocissus

P. quinquefolia (above & below)

Let a Virginia creeper adorn any garden that needs a look of wild abandon. Virginia creeper lights a wildfire of color each fall.

Growing

These vines grow well in any light from **full sun to full shade**. The soil should be **fertile** and **well drained**. The plants will adapt to clay or sandy soils.

Tips

Virginia creepers do not require support because they have clinging rootlets that adhere to just about any surface, including smooth wood, vinyl or metal. Give the plants lots of space and let them cover a wall, fence or arbor. They can also be used as groundcovers.

Recommended

These two species are very similar, except for the shape of the leaves. The **fruits** are **poisonous**.

P. quinquefolia (Virginia creeper, woodbine) has dark green foliage. Each leaf, divided into five leaflets, turns flaming red in fall.

P. tricuspidata (Boston ivy, Japanese creeper) has dark green, three-lobed leaves that turn red in fall. This species is not quite as hardy as *P. quinquefolia*.

Virginia creeper can cover the sides of buildings and help keep them cool in summer. Cut the plants back to keep windows and doors accessible.

Also called: Boston ivy **Features:** summer and fall foliage; clinging habit **Height:** 30–70' **Spread:** 30–70' **Hardiness:** zones 3–8

Wisteria

Wisteria

W. sinensis (above & below)

Loose clusters of purple hang like lace from the branches of wisteria. With prudent pruning, a gardener can create beautiful tree forms and arbor specimens.

Growing

Wisterias grow well in **full sun** or **partial shade**. The soil should be of **average fertility, moist** and **well drained**. Soil that is too fertile will produce lots of vegetative growth but very few flowers. Avoid planting wisterias near a lawn where fertilizer may leach over to your vines. Once established, they require less water.

To keep wisteria blooming sporadically all summer, prune off flowering spikes as soon as the flowers fade. A long-handled pole pruner works well. Wisteria will send out new blooming shoots until frost.

Tips

Wisteria requires something to twine around, such as an arbor or other sturdy structure. Select a permanent site; this vine doesn't like being moved. It may send up suckers, and it can root wherever branches touch the ground. Wisteria can become a heavy, thick plant, so trim and pinch as it grows to shape it.

Recommended

W. floribunda (Japanese wisteria) bears long, pendulous clusters of blue, purple, pink or white, fragrant flowers in late spring before the leaves emerge. Long, bean-like pods follow.

W. sinensis (Chinese wisteria) bears long, pendant clusters of blue-purple, fragrant flowers in late spring. **'Alba'** has white flowers.

All parts of wisteria are **poisonous**.

Features: late spring flowers; foliage; twining habit **Flower color:** blue, purple, pink, white **Height:** 20–50' or more **Spread:** 20–50' or more **Hardiness:** zones 4–8

Asiatic Lily

Lilium

Lilies in mixed planting (above), 'Stargazer' (below)

Asiatic lily produces decorative clusters of large, richly colored blooms at different times of the season depending on the hybrid. If you plant a variety of cultivars, you can have lilies blooming all season.

Growing

Lilies grow best in **full sun**, but they like to have their **roots shaded**. The soil should be **rich in organic matter, fertile, moist** and **well drained**.

Lily bulbs should be planted in fall before the first frost, but they can also be planted in spring if bulbs are available.

Tips

Lilies are often grouped in beds and borders and can be naturalized in woodland gardens and near water features. They look great in the back of a bed or in the center of a flower display. These plants are narrow but tall; plant at least three bulbs together to create some volume.

Recommended

The many species, hybrids and cultivars available are grouped by type. Check with your local garden center for what's available, or check online for some unusual varieties. **Asiatic hybrids** bear clusters of flowers in early or midsummer and are available in a wide range of colors. **Oriental hybrids** bear clusters of large, fragrant flowers in mid- and late summer. Colors are usually white, pink or red.

Lilies are poisonous if ingested.

Also called: Oriental lily **Features:** early, mid- or late season flowers in various colors **Flower color:** orange, yellow, peach, pink, purple, red, white **Height:** 24"–5' **Spread:** 12" **Hardiness:** zones 4–8

Crocosmia

Crocosmia

'Lucifer' (above), 'Norwich Canary' (below)

The intense colors of crocosmias are like beacons in the garden.

Growing

Crocosmias prefer **full sun** or **partial shade** in warmer regions. The soil should be of **average fertility, humus rich, moist** and **well drained**. Overgrown clumps produce few flowers.

Plant in a protected area and mulch in fall with shredded leaves or other organic matter to protect the roots from fluctuating winter temperatures. Near the coast and in well-drained soil, crocosmias will overwinter without additional winter protection.

Tips

Crocosmias look striking when massed in a herbaceous or mixed border. They also look good next to a pond, where the brightly colored flowers will be reflected in the water.

In cold winter areas, crocosmia corms can be dug up in fall and stored in slightly damp sawdust or peat moss in a cool, dark place. Monitor regularly. When they sprout, pot them and move them to a well-lit but cool room until planting out in spring.

Recommended

C.* × *crocosmiflora is a spreading plant with long, strap-like leaves and one-sided spikes of red, orange or yellow, mid- and late summer flowers. **'Citronella'** (golden fleece) bears bright yellow flowers.

***C.* 'Lucifer,'** the hardiest of the bunch, bears bright scarlet red flowers. Hummingbirds will love you for planting it.

Features: brightly colored flowers; strap-like foliage **Flower color:** shades of red, orange, yellow **Height:** 18"–4' **Spread:** 12–18" **Hardiness:** zones 5–8

Crocus

Crocus

Crocuses are harbingers of spring. Their bright, cheerful colors will melt away your winter blahs.

Growing

Crocuses grow well in **full sun** or **light shade**. The soil should be of **poor to average fertility, gritty** and **well drained**. Plant corms about 4" deep in fall.

Tips

Crocuses are almost always planted in groups. Drifts of crocuses planted in lawns provide early color while the grass remains dormant. In beds and borders they can be left to naturalize. Plants will fill in and spread out to provide a bright welcome in spring.

Try planting crocuses under deciduous trees and shrubs. They look great under the skirt of a weeping Japanese maple.

Features: early spring flowers **Flower color:** purple, yellow, white; also bicolored **Height:** 2–6" **Spread:** 2–4" **Hardiness:** zones 3–8

Recommended

Many crocus species, hybrids and cultivars are available. The familiar spring-flowering crocus is ***C.* × *vernus*** (Dutch crocus). Cultivars are available with flowers in shades of purple, yellow or white, sometimes bicolored or with darker veins.

Saffron is obtained from the dried, crushed stigmas of C. sativus. *It takes six plants to produce enough spice for one recipe. This fall-blooming plant is hardy to zone 6.*

Daffodil

Narcissus

Many gardeners automatically think of large, yellow, trumpet-shaped flowers when they think of daffodils, but there is a wide range of size, color and form among the many varieties. Daffodils perform well in a variety of climates and will tolerate both heat and cold.

Growing

Daffodils grow best in **full sun** or **light shade**. The soil should be **average to fertile, moist** and **well drained**.

Bulbs should be planted in late summer or early fall. The bigger the bulb, the deeper it should be planted. A rule of thumb is to measure the bulb from top to bottom and multiply that number by three to know how deep to plant.

Tips

Plant daffodils where they can be left to naturalize—in the light shade beneath a tree or in a woodland garden. In mixed beds and borders, the faded leaves are hidden by the summer foliage of other plants. Large-leaved perennials such as hosta and lady's mantle make fine companion plants.

Recommended

Many species, hybrids and cultivars of daffodils are available. Flowers may be borne solitary or in clusters. There are 12 different flower form categories.

The cup in the center of a daffodil is called the corona, and the group of petals and sepals that surrounds the corona is called the perianth.

Features: spring flowers **Flower color:** white, yellow, peach, orange, pink; also bicolored **Height:** 4–24" **Spread:** 4–12" **Hardiness:** zones 3–8

Dahlia

Dahlia

The variation in size, shape and color of dahlia flowers is astonishing. You are sure to find at least one that appeals to you.

Growing

Dahlias prefer **full sun** and **fertile, moist, well-drained** soil that is **rich in organic matter**. Deadhead to keep plants tidy and blooming.

Plant tubers in spring. Dig a large, deep hole for each tuber—the larger the flower, the larger the hole. Fill with a mix of organic matter and soil.

Tips

Dahlias make attractive, colorful additions to a mixed border. Smaller varieties are good edging plants, and larger ones make good alternatives to shrubs.

Where the ground freezes, dig up the tubers in fall and store them. If temperatures do not drop below 20°F, leave them in the ground and cover with mulch.

Recommended

Of the many dahlia hybrids, most are grown from tubers, but a few can be started from seed. Several hybrids are sold based on flower shape. The flowers are 2–12" across and are available in various colors. Attractive varieties with interesting and unusual flowers are also available.

Features: summer flowers; attractive foliage; bushy habit **Flower color:** purple, pink, white, yellow, orange, red; also bicolored **Height:** 8"–5' **Spread:** 8–18" **Hardiness:** tender perennials; grown as annuals in cooler regions

Flowering Onion

Allium

A. giganteum (above), *A. cernuum* (below)

Flowering onions, with their striking, ball-like or loose, nodding clusters of flowers, are sure to attract attention.

Growing

Flowering onions grow best in **full sun** or **partial shade** in hotter areas. The soil should be **average to fertile, moist** and **well drained**. Plant bulbs in late summer or early fall.

Tips

Flowering onions work best in groups in a bed or border where they can be left to naturalize. Most will self-seed when left to their own devices.

The foliage, which tends to fade just as the plants come into flower, can be hidden with groundcover or a low, bushy companion plant.

After flowering onions bloom, leave their flowerheads to dry on the stems. The dry flowers provide a starry feature all summer.

Recommended

Several flowering onion species, hybrids and cultivars have gained popularity for their decorative flowers. ***A. aflatunense*** has dense, globe-like clusters of lavender flowers. ***A. caeruleum*** (blue globe onion) bears globe-like clusters of blue flowers. ***A. cernuum*** (nodding onion, wild onion) has loose, drooping clusters of pink flowers. ***A. giganteum*** (giant onion) is a towering plant with large, globe-shaped clusters of pinky purple flowers.

Although its leaves have an onion scent when bruised, the flowers have a sweeter fragrance.

Features: summer flowers; cylindrical or strap-like leaves **Flower color:** pink, purple, white, yellow, blue, maroon **Height:** 12"–6' **Spread:** 2–12" **Hardiness:** zones 3–8

Snowdrop

Galanthus

When winter has you feeling dull and dreary, let early blooming snowdrops bring some much-needed color to your winter garden.

Growing

Snowdrops grow well in **full sun** or **partial shade** in **fertile, well-drained, moist, humus-rich** soil. Do not allow the soil to dry out in summer. Snowdrops do best in colder parts of the state.

Tips

Snowdrops work well in beds, borders and rock gardens. They should always be planted in groups and close to each other for the best effect. Snowdrops can be planted in the lawn or under deciduous shrubs and trees that will provide partial shade in summer. These plants are great for naturalizing in lightly shaded woodlands.

Recommended

G. elwesii (giant snowdrop) has larger flowers and foliage and grows taller than *G. nivalis*. The inner petals are heavily marked with green.

G. nivalis (common snowdrop) is a tiny plant that produces small, nodding, honey-scented, white flowers in mid- to late winter. The inner petals are marked with a green "V" shape. Cultivars are available, some with double flowers and some with yellow markings instead of green.

The various snowdrop species hybridize easily with each other; many hybrids are available.

Features: early blooming flowers; strap-like foliage; easy to grow **Flower color:** white **Height:** 4–12" **Spread:** 4–6" **Hardiness:** zones 3–8

G. elwesii with winter aconite (above), *G. nivalis* (below)

All parts of snowdrop are poisonous if ingested. Handling the bulbs may cause some irritation for people with sensitive skin.

Tulip

Tulipa

Tulips, with their beautifully colored flowers, are a welcome sight in the first warm days of spring. Tulips perform best in cooler areas.

Growing

Tulips grow best in **full sun**. The flowers tend to bend toward the light in partial or light shade. The soil should be **fertile** and **well drained**. Plant bulbs in fall. Cold-treated bulbs can be planted in spring.

To grow tulips in warmer areas, refrigerate bulbs in a paper bag for six weeks before planting in January. Drop some low-nitrogen fertilizer in the planting hole. Water thoroughly immediately after planting, then sparingly until leaves emerge. After that, provide regular water.

When choosing tulip bulbs, remember: the bigger the bulb, the bigger the bloom.

Tips

Tulips provide the best display when mass planted in flowerbeds and borders. They can also be grown in containers and forced to bloom early in indoor pots. Some tulips can be naturalized in meadow and wildflower gardens.

Recommended

There are about 100 species of tulips and thousands of hybrids and cultivars. They are generally divided into 15 groups based on bloom time and flower appearance. Tulips come in dozens of shades, with many bicolored and multi-colored varieties. Blue is the only color not available. Purchase your tulips in early fall for the best selection. Although tulips can repeat bloom, many hybrids perform best if planted new each year. Species and older cultivars are the best choice for naturalizing.

Features: spring flowers **Flower color:** all colors except blue **Height:** 6–30" **Spread:** 2–8" **Hardiness:** zones 3–8; often grown as an annual

Basil

Ocimum

The sweet, fragrant leaves of fresh basil add a delicious flavor to salads and tomato-based dishes.

Growing

Basil grows best in a **warm, sheltered** location in **full sun**. The soil should be **fertile, moist** and **well drained**. Pinch tips regularly to encourage bushy growth.

Tips

Although basil will grow best in a warm spot outdoors in the garden, it can be grown successfully indoors in a pot by a bright window to provide you with fresh leaves all year.

Recommended

O. basilicum is one of the most popular culinary herbs. There are dozens of varieties, including ones with large or tiny, green or purple and smooth or ruffled leaves. Cultivars of varying height are also available.

'Genovese' & 'Cinnamon' (above), 'Genovese' (below)

Basil is a good companion plant for tomatoes—both like warm, moist growing conditions, and when you pick tomatoes for a salad, you'll also remember to include a few leaves of basil.

Features: fragrant, decorative, edible leaves **Height:** 6–24" **Spread:** 6–18" **Hardiness:** tender annual

Chives

Allium

A. schoenoprasum (above & below)

The delicate onion flavor of chives is best enjoyed fresh. Mix chives into dips or sprinkle them onto salads and baked potatoes. The blooms are striking in the garden and in herbal vinegars.

Growing

Chives grow well in **full sun** or **partial shade**. The soil should be **fertile, moist** and **well drained**, but chives adapt to most soil conditions. Young leaves are the most tender and flavorful, so cut back plants to encourage new growth if flavor diminishes.

Tips

Chives are decorative enough to be included in a mixed or herbaceous border and can be left to naturalize. In a herb garden, chives should be given plenty of space to allow self-seeding.

Recommended

A. schoenoprasum forms a clump of bright green, cylindrical leaves. Clusters of pinky purple flowers are produced in early and midsummer. Varieties with white or pink flowers are available.

A. tuberosum (garlic chives) have a distinct garlic flavor and self-seed more readily than other types.

Chives will spread with reckless abandon as the clumps grow larger and the plants self-seed.

Features: foliage; form; flowers **Flower color:** pink, purple, white **Height:** 8–24" **Spread:** 12" or more **Hardiness:** zones 3–8

Coriander • Cilantro

Coriandrum

Coriander is a multi-purpose herb. The leaves, called cilantro, are used in salads, salsas and soups. The seeds, called coriander, are used in pies, chutneys and marmalades. Each has a distinct flavor.

Growing

Coriander prefers **full sun** but benefits from partial shade in the heat of summer. Too much heat may cause bolting. The soil should be **fertile, light** and **well drained**. This plant dislikes humid conditions and does best during a dry summer.

Tips

Coriander has pungent leaves and is best planted where people will not have to brush past it. It is, however, a delight to behold when in flower. Add a plant or two throughout your borders and vegetable garden, both for the visual appeal and to attract beneficial insects.

Recommended

C. sativum forms a clump of lacy basal foliage above which large, loose clusters of tiny, white flowers are produced. The seeds ripen in late summer and fall.

The delicate, cloud-like clusters of flowers attract pollinating insects such as butterflies and bees as well as abundant predatory insects that will help keep pest insects to a minimum.

Features: form; foliage; flowers; seeds **Flower color:** white **Height:** 16–24" **Spread:** 8–16" **Hardiness:** tender annual

Lavender

Lavandula

L. angustifolia (above & below)

Lavender is a beautiful aromatic plant that is a welcome addition to any sunny garden. Lavender has antibacterial and antifungal properties and a sharp, clean scent. Its essential oil can relax yet energize the nervous system.

Growing

Lavenders grow best in **full sun** in very **well-drained, alkaline**, **average to fertile** soil. Established plants are heat and drought tolerant. They perform well in many parts of California.

L. × *intermedia* can be sensitive to winter cold and should be planted out of winter winds. In colder areas, cover lavenders with mulch and a good layer of snow. Good drainage is essential to winter survival—often, winterkill results from wet feet, not from cold.

Tips

Lavenders are deer-resistant and can be used as edging plants and in low hedges. Plant them with other drought-tolerant specimens such as pinks and thyme.

Recommended

L. angustifolia (English lavender) is an aromatic, bushy sub-shrub that is often treated as a perennial. It bears spikes of small flowers in shades of violet-blue. Cultivars come in different sizes, with flowers in shades of purple, blue and pink.

L.* × *intermedia (lavandin) is a hybrid of English lavender and spike lavender *(L. latifolia)*. The flowers are held on long spikes.

Visit your local garden center to discover what types do best in your region.

Overwatering drowns lavender plants. In coastal regions, water immediately after planting; then allow your lavender to thrive on rainfall alone.

Features: fragrance; summer to fall flowers; foliage **Flower color:** shades of purple, blue, pink **Height:** 8–36" **Spread:** up to 4' **Hardiness:** zones 5–9

Mint

Mentha

Prized for its spicy-sweet leaves, mint can be invasive. Corral its enthusiasm in a container. The fragrant leaves may smell like apple, pineapple or chocolate.

Various mints (above), *M.* × *gracilis* 'Variegata' (below)

Growing

Mint grows well in **full sun** or **partial shade**. The soil should be **average to fertile, humus rich** and **moist**. Mint spreads vigorously by rhizomes and may need a barrier in the soil to restrict its spread. To plant it directly in the garden, leave it in a plastic container with the bottom removed. Pinch to control growth and promote bushiness.

Tips

Mint is delightful but invasive. Try growing it in a container of mixed herbs to keep it in bounds. The flowers attract bees, butterflies and other pollinators to the garden.

Recommended

There are many species, hybrids and cultivars of mint. ***M. spicata*** (spearmint), ***M.* × *piperita*** (peppermint) and ***M.* × *piperita citrata*** (orange mint) are three of the most commonly grown culinary varieties. More decorative varieties with variegated or curly leaves as well as varieties with unusual, fruit-scented leaves are also available.

***M.* × *gracilis* 'Variegata'** (variegated ginger mint) has attractive, bright green and gold variegated foliage that has a strong, fruity mint aroma and ginger flavor.

A few sprigs of fresh mint added to a pitcher of iced tea gives the tea an added zip.

Features: fragrant foliage; summer flowers **Flower color:** purple, pink, white **Height:** 6–36" **Spread:** 36" or more **Hardiness:** zones 4–8

Oregano • Marjoram

Origanum

O. vulgare 'Polyphant' (above), *O. vulgare* 'Aureum' (below)

Oregano and marjoram are two of the best known and most frequently used herbs. They are popular in stuffings, soups and stews, and no pizza is complete until it's sprinkled with fresh or dried oregano leaves.

Growing

Oregano and marjoram grow best in **full sun**. The soil should be of **poor to average fertility, neutral to alkaline** and **well drained**. They are somewhat drought tolerant once established, and keeping them on the dry side concentrates flavor. New wood is most productive, so cut them back in winter.

Tips

These bushy perennials make a lovely addition to any border and can be trimmed to form low hedges. Low-growing oregano does well in rock gardens and looks especially attractive combined with variegated and golden sage. The flowers attract pollinators to the garden.

Recommended

O. majorana (marjoram) is an upright plant with light green, hairy leaves. It produces white or pink flowers in summer and can be grown as an annual where it is not hardy.

O. vulgare hirtum (oregano, Greek oregano) is the most flavorful culinary variety. It is low growing and has hairy, gray-green leaves and white flowers. Many interesting varieties are available with golden, variegated or curly leaves.

In Greek, oros *means "mountain" and* ganos *means "joy," so oregano translates as "joy of the mountain."*

Features: fragrant, edible foliage; summer flowers; bushy habit **Flower color:** white, pink **Height:** 12–32" **Spread:** 8–18" **Hardiness:** zones 5–8

Parsley

Petroselinum

Although usually used as a garnish, parsley is rich in vitamins and minerals and is reputed to freshen the breath after garlic or onion-rich foods are eaten.

Growing

Parsley grows well in **full sun** or **partial shade**. The soil should be of **average to rich drained**.

Parsley resents transplanting and should be started where you mean to grow it. Soaking the seeds for 24 hours prior to planting improves germination. Nursery-grown container plants are readily available.

Tips

Containers of parsley can be kept close to the house for easy picking. The bright foliage and compact growth habit make parsley a good edging plant for beds and borders.

Features: attractive foliage **Height:** 8–24" **Spread:** 12–24" **Hardiness:** zones 5–8; often grown as an annual

Recommended

P. crispum forms a clump of bright green, divided leaves. This plant is a biennial usually grown as an annual. Cultivars may have flat or curly leaves. Flat leaves are more flavorful; curly leaves are more decorative. Dwarf cultivars are available.

Parsley leaves make a tasty and nutritious addition to salads. Shred freshly picked leaves and sprinkle them over your mixed greens.

Rosemary

Rosmarinus

Cut woody spears of rosemary and use them as skewers for barbecuing meat.

Rosemary's needle-like leaves are used to flavor a wide variety of culinary dishes, including chicken, pork, lamb, rice, tomato and egg dishes. A Mediterranean native, this versatile herb performs well under a variety of conditions and has great value as a landscape plant.

Growing

Rosemary prefers **full sun** but tolerates partial shade. The soil should be of **poor to average fertility** and **well drained**. Rosemary thrives on a bit of neglect; be stingy with water and fertilizer.

In cold areas, shelter it from winter winds. Remove the woody branches to encourage fresh new growth.

Tips

Grow rosemary in shrub borders where it's hardy, or plant it in a container as a specimen. Low-growing, spreading plants can be included in rock gardens, along the top of retaining walls or in hanging baskets.

Rosemary attracts birds, butterflies and bees.

Recommended

R. officinalis is a dense, bushy, evergreen shrub with narrow, dark green leaves. Cultivar habits vary from strongly upright to prostrate and spreading. Flowers usually come in shades of blue, but pink-flowered cultivars are available. Some cultivars can survive in zone 6 in a sheltered location with winter protection. Plants rarely reach their mature size when grown in containers.

Features: fragrant, evergreen foliage; summer flowers **Flower color:** bright blue, sometimes pink **Height:** 8"–4' **Spread:** 12"–4' **Hardiness:** zone 8

Sage

Salvia

Sage is perhaps the best-known flavoring for stuffing, but it has a great range of uses, including in soups, stews, sausages and dumplings.

Growing

Sage prefers **full sun** but tolerates light shade. The soil should be of **average fertility** and **well drained**. These plants benefit from a light mulching with compost each year. They are drought tolerant once established.

Tips

Sage is an attractive plant for a border; it adds volume to the middle of the border and makes an attractive edging or feature plant near the front. Sage can also be grown in mixed planters and is a long-lived standard in rock gardens.

Recommended

S. officinalis is a woody, mounding plant with soft, gray-green leaves. Spikes of light purple flowers appear in early and midsummer. Many cultivars with attractive foliage are available, including the silver-leaved **'Berggarten,'** the yellow-margined **'Icterina,'** the purple-leaved **'Purpurea'** and the cream variegated **'Tricolor,'** which has a pink flush to the new growth.

'Icternia' (above), 'Purpurea' (below)

Sage has been used since at least ancient Greek times as a medicinal and culinary herb and continues to be widely used for both those purposes today.

Features: fragrant, decorative, edible foliage; summer flowers **Flower color:** blue, purple **Height:** 12–24" **Spread:** 18–36" **Hardiness:** zones 5–8

Thyme

Thymus

'Lanuginosis' (above), *T.* × *citriodorus* (below)

Thyme is a popular culinary herb used in soups, stews and casseroles, and with roasts.

Thyme is a member of the mint family.

Growing

Thyme prefers **full sun**. The soil should be **neutral to alkaline** and of **poor to average fertility**. Very **good drainage** is essential. It is beneficial to work some leaf mold into the soil. Thyme tolerates some drought once established.

Once plants finish flowering, shear them back by about half to encourage new growth and to prevent the plants from becoming too woody.

Tips

Thyme works well in sunny, dry locations at the front of borders, between or beside paving stones, on rock gardens and rock walls, and in containers. Creeping thyme makes a good lawn substitute.

Recommended

T.* × *citriodorus (lemon-scented thyme) forms a mound of lemon-scented, dark green foliage with pale pink flowers. Cultivars with silver- or gold-margined leaves are available.

T. praecox* subsp. *arcticus (*T. serpyllum*, mother of thyme, creeping thyme, wild thyme) is a low-growing variety with purple flowers. Many cultivars are available. **'Elfin'** forms tiny, dense mounds of foliage. **'Lanuginosis'** (woolly thyme) is mat forming with fuzzy, gray-green leaves and pink or purple flowers.

T. vulgaris (common thyme) forms a bushy mound of dark green leaves and purple, pink or white flowers. Cultivars with variegated leaves are available.

Features: bushy habit; fragrant, decorative, edible foliage; flowers **Flower color:** purple, pink, white **Height:** 2–16" **Spread:** 4–16" **Hardiness:** zones 4–8

Black Mondo Grass

Ophiopogon

'Nigrescens' (above), 'Ebknizam' (below)

Black mondo grass is an excellent accent and contrast plant. A black background highlights any brightly colored plants or flowers.

Growing

Black mondo grass prefers to grow in **full sun** or **light shade** in **moist, moderately fertile, well-drained, humus-rich** soil. The foliage is at its best in full sun. Divide in spring just as new growth resumes. These plants appreciate some winter protection of thick mulch in zones 5 and 6.

Tips

Because it spreads by rhizomes, black mondo grass can be used as a dense groundcover and for erosion control. Use it for border edges and containers. It can also be used as a bedding plant in cooler zones, and can be dug up and stored for winter in a cool, dark room.

This plant is a member of the lily family and does not like being mowed.

Recommended

***O. planiscapus* 'Ebknizam'** ('Ebony Night') has curving, almost black leaves and dark lavender flowers. It grows 4–6" tall and 6–12" wide. **'Nigrescens'** has curving, almost black foliage and pink to white-flushed pink flowers. It grows 6–12" tall and 12" wide. Both cultivars produce blackish, berry-like fruit.

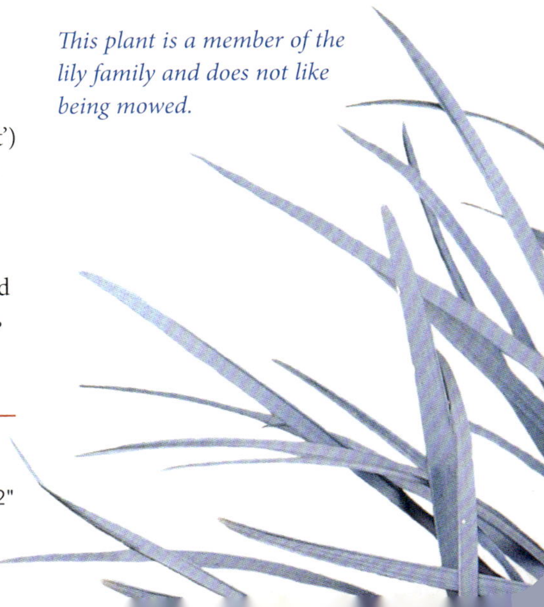

Also called: black lilyturf **Features:** uniquely colored foliage **Flower color:** lavender, pink, white-flushed pink **Height:** 4–12" **Spread:** 6–12" **Hardiness:** zones 5–9

Blue Fescue

Festuca

'Elijah Blue' (above), *F. glauca* (below)

Blue fescue was one of the first ornamental grasses to appear on the market, and it continues to display its finest features in harsh conditions.

Growing

Fescue prefers **full sun** in **poor to moderately fertile, well-drained** soil. Keep the soil a little on the **dry** side.

Fescue specimens can be divided every two to three years or when they begin to die out in the centers. This will help to maintain the foliage color.

Tips

The low-growing tufts of blue fescue are used as edging for beds and borders, and they look great mass planted. Fescue is frequently used in xeriscape settings and naturalized areas. Low-growing blue fescue also works well in rock and alpine gardens. In warmer areas, it lasts for about two years before it needs to be replaced.

Recommended

F. glauca produces steely blue tufts of fine, needle-like blades of grass. Most varieties produce tan-colored flower spikes that rise above the mounds of blue foliage. A great many cultivars and hybrids are available. **'Elijah Blue'** has soft, powdery blue foliage.

Features: colorful foliage; flower spikes; growth habit
Height: 6–18" **Spread:** 10–12" **Hardiness:** zones 3–8

Golden Hakone Grass

Hakonechloa

Golden hakone grass is one of the most beautiful ornamental grasses available. The striking foliage cascades nicely over the edges of containers or low borders.

Growing

Golden hakone grass grows well in **partial shade** or **light shade** in **moist, well-drained, moderately fertile, humus-rich** soil. The leaf color is enhanced in partial to light shade; golden hakone can tolerate full shade, but its foliage will turn lime green under such conditions. It also tolerates full sun in cooler areas, but keep the soil moist. Divide in spring. Avoid locations with cold, drying winds.

Tips

Golden hakone grass works well at the edge of a woodland garden, but is also very effective in containers, beds, borders and rock gardens. It makes an excellent addition to larger gardens where it can be planted in drifts.

Recommended

***H. macra* 'Aureola'** is a slow-spreading, mound-forming, perennial grass with lush, cascading foliage. It has yellow foliage with narrow green stripes. The foliage adopts a bronze to pinkish red tint in fall before it dies back in winter. The variegated cultivars are more popular than the species.

This slow-growing grass is very well behaved and will not invade its neighbors.

Also called: Japanese forest grass
Features: colorful, decorative, strap-like foliage; fall color **Height:** 10–18"
Spread: 30–36" **Hardiness:** zones 5–9

Japanese Painted Fern

Athyrium

'Pictum' (above & below)

Japanese painted ferns are striking plants that add wonderful color to an otherwise shady green landscape.

Growing

Japanese painted fern requires **partial shade** to maintain its colorful foliage. If it is planted in full shade, the color may not develop, whereas full sun will cause the color to fade or the leaves to scorch. The soil should be **moderately fertile, moist, neutral to acidic** and **humus rich**. Divide in spring when necessary.

Plants grown from spores show more varied foliage coloration that those grown from divisions.

It is important to apply a thick layer of mulch in fall to maintain a better moisture level around the roots and to protect the crown from exposure.

Tips

Japanese painted fern looks very attractive planted en masse in mixed borders or shade gardens. The interesting foliage stands out among other ferns in a woodland setting.

Recommended

A. nipponicum is a creeping, compact fern that bears long, mid-green fronds with reddish purple midribs. The cultivars are far more readily available and attractive than the species. They come in a variety of foliage colors, with new additions yearly.

Features: attractive foliage **Height:** 12–24" **Spread:** 12–24" **Hardiness:** zones 4–8

Japanese Silver Grass

Miscanthus

One of the most widely grown ornamental grasses available, Japanese silver grass offers vivid colors and ornamental plumes, and it needs little maintenance. There is a vast array of species and cultivars.

'Purpurascens' (above), 'Zebrinus' (below)

Growing

Japanese silver grass grows well in **full sun** or partial shade in moderately **moist, fertile, well-drained** soil, but it will tolerate a variety of conditions.

Tips

Japanese silver grass is most effective when massed in a naturalized area or mixed border. Some varieties can grow quite large and are best displayed as specimens. If left alone in fall and winter, the dried foliage and showy plumes are very attractive.

Recommended

M. sinensis is a perennial, clumping grass. Its many cultivars and hybrids offer variegated, striped or speckled foliage of one or more colors and tall, ornate, persistent plumes. **'Morning Light'** grows 4–5' tall and 3–4' wide and bears green foliage edged with white and reddish bronze flowers.

The fan-shaped plumes are ideal for cutting for use in crafts and in fresh and dried arrangements.

Also called: Chinese silver grass, Eulalia grass, maiden grass **Features:** colorful, decorative, strap-like foliage and showy plumes; winter interest **Height:** 3–8' **Spread:** 2–4' **Hardiness:** zones 3–8

Maidenhair Fern

Adiantum

Maidenhair fern is often found growing in shady, moist locations beside streams or creeks. It is a non-invasive plant that spreads slowly and looks good planted with other shade-loving plants such as astilbe, fringed bleeding heart, hosta, lungwort and toad lily.

Growing

Maidenhair fern prefers **partial to full shade** and **moist, well-drained, fertile** soil.

This fern is easy to propagate in fall. Just slice off a section of the thick root mass and replant it in a cool spot.

Tips

Maidenhair fern works best at the edge of a woodland garden. It makes a good addition to a shaded border or a shaded rock garden. Maidenhair fern also does well in a streamside planting.

Recommended

A. pedatum (northern maidenhair fern) is a deciduous, upright plant that bears branched, horizontally oriented, lance-shaped fronds and lobed, fan-shaped, mid-green foliage that turns yellow-green to yellow in fall. The leaflets have a waxy coating that rapidly sheds water and raindrops. The stems are dark brown to black.

Adiantium *species have been used to cure bronchitis, coughs and asthma. They are also known as hair tonics and restoratives.*

Features: attractive foliage **Height:** 12–24" **Spread:** 12–24" **Hardiness:** zones 3–8

Ostrich Fern

Matteuccia

These easy-to-grow ferns are appreciated as much for their delicious, emerging spring fronds as for their ornamental foliage and habit.

Growing

Ostrich fern prefers **partial shade** or **light shade** but tolerates full shade. It can take full sun in cooler climates, provided the soil remains moist. Soil should be **average to fertile, humus rich, neutral to acidic** and **moist**. Divide in spring.

Tips

This fern appreciates a moist woodland garden and is often found growing wild along the edges of woodland streams and creeks. Useful in shaded borders, these plants are quick to spread, to the delight of those who have tasted the delicate young fronds.

Recommended

M. struthiopteris (*M. pensylvanica*) forms a circular cluster of slightly arching fronds. Stiff, brown, fertile fronds poke up in the center of the cluster in late summer and persist through winter.

The new spring fronds are tightly coiled in the shape of fiddleheads and taste delicious when lightly steamed and served with butter. Remove the bitter, reddish brown papery coating before steaming.

Also called: fiddlehead fern **Features:** foliage; habit **Height:** 3–5' **Spread:** 12–36" or more **Hardiness:** zones 2–8

Phormium

Phormium

P. tenax 'Purpureum' (above), *P. tenax* cultivar (below)

These bold, impressive plants create quite an impact. They will become the focal point of any planting.

Growing

Phormium grows best in **full sun** in **well-drained** soil. Phormium adapts to a variety of conditions. *P. cookianum* and *P.* hybrids (*P. cookianum* × *P. tenax*) appreciate shade from the hot afternoon sun.

Temperatures below 20° F often damage the evergreen foliage, but it will regrow from the rhizome in spring. A layer of thick mulch helps protect the rhizomes in winter.

Tips

Use phormium in beds, borders and container plantings. It looks good near entryways and walkways.

Recommended

There is a wide selection of available species, hybrids and cultivars. These plants have broad, strap-shaped leaves that come in a wide variety of colors. Many plants mature at over 6' tall with equal spreads, but when grown as annuals they rarely get this big. In warmer parts of California, they are evergreen perennials. Dwarf cultivars that grow to about 24" tall are also available. Plants with bronze foliage are the hardiest selections.

Also called: New Zealand flax **Features:** green, black, red or yellow, often multicolored and striped foliage **Height:** 2–8' **Spread:** 2–8' **Hardiness:** zones 8–10

Purple Fountain Grass

Pennisetum

Purple fountain grass makes a striking impact, especially when it anchors a container planting.

'Rubrum' (above & below)

Growing

Purple fountain grass grows best in **full sun** in **light, well-drained, moderately fertile** soil.

Purple fountain grass can be dug up, brought inside and stored in a cool room for winter. If it has been grown in a container, cut back the foliage in fall and store the whole container. Make sure the root mass remains moist. This plant's seeds are sterile, and it must be propagated vegetatively.

Tips

This ornamental grass can be planted in beds and borders, en masse, as a specimen or accent plant, or in a rock garden.

Recommended

***P. setaceum* 'Rubrum'** ('Purpureum') is a dense, mound-forming, tender perennial grass that grows 3–5' tall and 18–36" wide. It has narrow, dark purple foliage and large, showy, rose red flower spikes from midsummer to fall. **'Burgundy Giant'** can grow 6' tall and 2–4' wide, and has wide, deep burgundy purple foliage. Its nodding flower spikes are pinkish purple and up to 15" long. It is hardy to zone 10.

The foliage of purple fountain grass turns brown and dry in winter and can be a fire hazard.

Features: colorful foliage; large, fuzzy flower spikes; graceful habit **Height:** 2–6' **Spread:** 18"–4' **Hardiness:** zones 9–10

Reed Grass

Calamagrostis

'Karl Foerster' (above & below)

Reed grass is one of the first ornamental grasses to grow and bloom. It is highly sought after and frequently used by landscape designers, who appreciate its upright form and early growth.

Growing

Reed grass thrives in **full sun** or **partial shade** in **moist, humus-rich, well-drained** soil. It is tolerant of dry soils, wet soils, clay soils, heat and drought.

Cut the plant back to about 3–4" above the ground in late winter to early spring before the new growth begins. Divide in spring.

Tips

Reed grass works best as a vertical accent plant in beds, borders and containers.

Recommended

C. × acutiflora is a slow-growing, upright perennial grass with arching, narrow, green foliage and tall, wiry stems that bear silvery bronze to pinkish purple panicles of flowers. Decorative cultivars are available in varied sizes and colors. **'Karl Foerster'** was the Perennial Plant Association's 2001 Plant of the Year.

Reed grass seeds slowly shatter in late fall and early winter. The flower stems they leave behind are less attractive over winter than most upright ornamental grasses.

Also called: smallweed, feather reed grass **Features:** decorative flower stems, foliage, habit **Height:** 2–6' **Spread:** 12–24" **Hardiness:** zones 4–8

Rush

Juncus

Rush is often mistaken for a grass. The stems are hollow and cylindrical rather than flat and broad like grass leaves. This unique plant is a must for any water garden.

'Spiralis' (above & below)

Growing

Rush grows best in **full sun** or **partial shade**. The soil should be consistently **moist to wet**, and **slightly acidic**.

Tips

Rush is well suited to bog gardens, water gardens and locations that remain moist for long periods. It can be grown in a small container and/ or submerged in water up to the crown in a water feature or pond.

Recommended

J. effusus is a perennial, clump-forming, wetland plant that has slightly arching stems and spreads by vigorous underground rhizomes. **'Cuckoo'** has longitudinal yellow stripes. **'Spiralis'** (corkscrew rush) is low-growing rush with curly, spiraling stems. **'Unicorn'** is an exaggerated version of 'Spiralis,' with thicker, longer, curled stems. **'Zebrinus'** has broad white bands.

Rush cultivars can overwinter outdoors in the colder areas of our region if they are buried in a well-protected, moist area and covered with several inches of bark mulch or leaf matter. They can also be brought indoors and treated as houseplants until they return outdoors in spring.

Features: foliage; form **Height:** 12"–4'
Spread: 12–36" **Hardiness:** zones 2–9

Sedge

Carex

'Frosted Curls' (above), *C. morrowii* 'Variegata' (below)

"Sedges have edges" is the opening line to a classic gardener's poem that describes this plant as having triangular stems, unlike the true grasses. Sedge foliage comes in green, blue, rust, bronze and gold, and allows the gardener to add broad, colorful strokes or bright accents to the landscape.

Growing

Most sedges grow well in **full sun** or **partial shade** in **moist, well-drained, neutral to slightly alkaline** soil. 'Frosted Curls' prefers average to dry soil and is drought tolerant once established.

Stems can be cut to the ground in early spring before new growth occurs, or they can be "combed" to remove older foliage.

Propagate by seed or division of clumps in mid-spring to early summer.

Tips

Use the colorful foliage and rustic texture of these grass-like plants in rock gardens, water features, containers and borders. The fine foliage of 'Frosted Curls' contrasts well with coarse-textured plants.

Recommended

There are many sedges available; check your local garden center. ***C. comans* 'Frosted Curls'** (*C.* 'Frosted Curls'; New Zealand hair sedge) is a compact, clump-forming, evergreen perennial with fine-textured, very pale green, weeping foliage. The foliage appears almost iridescent, with unusual curled and twisted tips.

For seed collecting, allow seedheads to dry on the plants, then remove and collect the seeds.

Features: interesting, colorful foliage; growth habit **Height:** 10–18" **Spread:** 12–15" **Hardiness:** zones 7–9 (may grow successfully in zone 6, given favorable conditions)

Glossary

Acid soil: soil with a pH lower than 7.0

Annual: a plant that germinates, flowers, sets seed and dies in one growing season

Alkaline soil: soil with a pH higher than 7.0

Basal leaves: leaves that form from the crown, at the base of the plant

Bract: a modified leaf at the base of a flower or flower cluster

Corm: a bulblike, food-storing, underground stem, resembling a bulb without scales

Crown: the part of the plant at or just below soil level where the shoots join the roots

Cultivar: a cultivated plant variety with one or more distinct differences from the species, e.g., in flower color or disease resistance

Damping off: fungal disease causing seedlings to rot at soil level and topple over

Deadhead: to remove spent flowers to maintain a neat appearance and encourage a longer blooming season

Direct sow: to sow seeds directly in the garden

Dormancy: a period of plant inactivity, usually during winter or unfavorable conditions

Double flower: a flower with an unusually large number of petals

Genus: a category of biological classification between the species and family levels; the first word in a scientific name indicates the genus

Grafting: a type of propagation in which a stem or bud of one plant is joined onto the rootstock of another plant of a closely related species

Hardy: capable of surviving unfavorable conditions, such as cold weather or frost, without protection

Hip: the fruit of a rose, containing the seeds

Humus: decomposed or decomposing organic material in the soil

Hybrid: a plant resulting from natural or human-induced cross-breeding between varieties, species or genera

Inflorescence: a flower cluster

Neutral soil: soil with a pH of 7.0

Perennial: a plant that takes three or more years to complete its life cycle

pH: a measure of acidity or alkalinity; the soil pH influences availability of nutrients for plants

Rhizome: a root-like, food-storing stem that grows horizontally at or just below soil level, from which new shoots may emerge

Rootball: the root mass and surrounding soil of a plant

Seedhead: dried, inedible fruit that contains seeds; the fruiting stage of the inflorescense

Self-seeding: reproducing by means of seeds without human assistance, so that new plants constantly replace those that die

Semi-double flower: a flower with petals in two or three rings

Single flower: a flower with a single ring of typically four or five petals

Species: the fundamental unit of biological classification; the entity from which cultivars and varieties are derived

Standard: a shrub or small tree grown with an erect main stem, accomplished either through pruning and training or by grafting the plant onto a tall, straight stock

Sucker: a shoot that comes up from the root, often some distance from the plant; it can be separated to form a new plant once it develops its own roots

Tender: incapable of surviving the climatic conditions of a given region and requiring protection from frost or cold

Tuber: the thick section of a rhizome bearing nodes and buds

Variegation: foliage that has more than one color, often patched or striped or bearing leaf margins of a different color

Variety: a naturally occurring variant of a species

Index of Common Names and Genera